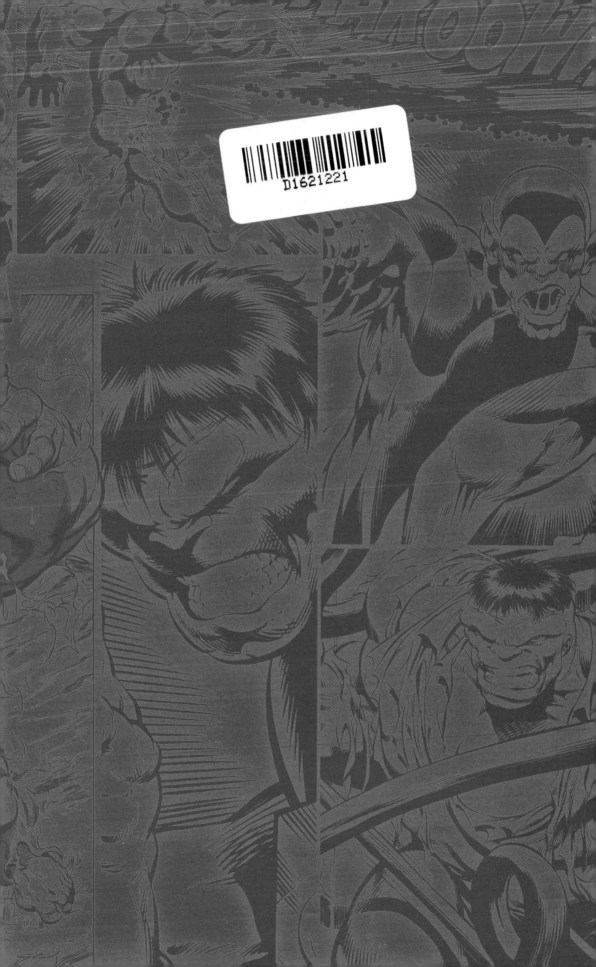

THE INCREDIBLE HULK™

SILENT SCREAMS

Reader Services

CUSTOMER SERVICE IN THE UK AND REPUBLIC OF IRELAND
How to continue your collection:
Customers can either place an order with their newsagent or receive issues on subscription.
Back issues: Either order through your newsagent or write to: Marvel Collection, Jacklin Enterprises UK, PO Box 77, Jarrow, NE32 3YH, enclosing payment of the cover price plus £1.00 p&p per copy. (Republic of Ireland: cover price plus €1.75).
Subscriptions: You can have your issues sent directly to your home. For details, see insert in issue 1 or phone our Customer Service Hotline on 0871 472 4240 (Monday to Friday, 9am-5pm, calls cost 10p per minute from UK landline). Alternatively you can write to Marvel Collection, Jacklin Enterprises UK, PO Box 77, Jarrow, NE32 3YH, or fax your enquiries to 0871 472 4241, or e-mail: marvelcollection@jacklinservice.com or visit www.graphicnovelcollection.com

CUSTOMER SERVICE IN OVERSEAS MARKETS

Australia: Back issues can be ordered from your newsagent. Alternatively telephone (03) 9872 4000 or write to:
Back Issues Department, Bissett Magazine Services, PO Box 3460, Nunawading Vic 3131. Please enclose payment of the cover price, plus A$2.49 (inc. GST) per issue postage and handling. Back issues are subject to availability.
Subscriptions: You can have your issues sent directly to your home. For details, see insert in issue 1 or phone our Customer Service Hotline on (03) 9872 4000. Alternatively you can write to Hachette subs offer, Bissett Magazine Services, PO Box 3460, Nunawading Vic 3131, or fax your enquiries to (03) 9873 4988, or order online at www.bissettmags.com.au

New Zealand: For back issues, ask your local magazine retailer or write to: Netlink, PO Box 47906, Ponsonby, Auckland.
South Africa: Back issues are available through your local CNA store or other newsagent.
Subscriptions: call (011) 265 4309, fax (011) 314 2984, or write to: Marvel Collection, Private Bag 10, Centurion 0046 or e-mail: service@jacklin.co.za
Malta: Back issues are only available through your local newsagent.
Malaysia: Call (03) 8023 3260, or e-mail: sales@allscript.com
Singapore: Call (65) 287 7090, or e-mail: sales@allscript.com

Published by Hachette Partworks Ltd, Jordan House, 47 Brunswick Place, London, N1 6EB
www.hachettepartworks.co.uk

Distributed in the UK and Republic of Ireland by Marketforce

This special edition published in 2012 by Hachette Partworks Ltd. forming part of The Ultimate Marvel Graphic Novel Collection.

Licensed by Marvel Characters B.V. through Panini S.p.A., Italy. All Rights Reserved.

Printed in China.
ISBN: 978-1-906965-70-9

THE INCREDIBLE HULK ™

PETER DAVID
WRITER

DALE KEOWN
PENCILS

BOB MCLEOD
INKS

GLYNIS OLIVER
COLOURS

JOE ROSEN & SAM DE LA ROSA
LETTERS

BOBBIE CHASE
EDITOR

TOM DEFALCO
EDITOR IN CHIEF

THE INCREDIBLE HULK:
SILENT SCREAMS

Marco M. Lupoi
*Panini Publishing Director
(Europe)*

To the public at large, the traditional image of the Hulk is of a simple-minded, green-skinned, rampaging behemoth with a penchant for extreme property damage, but dedicated comic fans know there is more to Bruce Banner's gamma-spawned alter ego than this. These days he is as subtly nuanced as any of Marvel's creations with a rich depth of personality far removed from his 'monster movie' origins.

Of all the Hulk's many writers, the one responsible for bringing real definition to the character is Peter David. For nearly 10 years he wrote what many fans regard as the definitive run on the title. He fleshed out both Banner and the Hulk and found innovative new ways to highlight the constant internal struggle between the two. Probably his greatest idea was to view Banner's condition through the eyes of a psychologist, developing the concept that the Hulk's genesis lay with his childhood trauma and subsequent multiple personality disorder.

Though it represents only a small snapshot of Peter David's Hulk work, *Silent Screams* contains all the action, emotion and humour his stories are famous for. If you're not already a fan of the jade-giant, we guarantee you will be by the time you finish this volume!

Contains material originally published in magazine form as The Incredible Hulk #370-377. Senior Editor (Hachette Partworks Ltd.), Sarah Gale. Packaged by Panini Publishing, a division of Panini UK Limited. Mike Riddell, Managing Director. Alan O'Keefe, Managing Editor. Ed Hammond, Editor. Marco M. Lupoi, Publishing Director Europe. Tim Warran-Smith, Designer. Additional content: Mike Conroy. Office of publication: Brockbourne House, 77 Mount Ephraim, Tunbridge Wells, Kent TN4 8BS. No similarity between any of the names, characters, persons and/or institutions in this edition with those of any living or dead person or institution is intended, and any such similarity which may exist is purely coincidental. This publication may not be sold, except by authorised dealers, and is sold subject to the condition that it shall not be sold or distributed with any part of its cover or markings removed, nor in a mutilated condition.

THE STORY SO FAR...

Events leading up to The Incredible Hulk: Silent Screams

Caught in the blast of a gamma-bomb explosion, Bruce Banner now finds himself transformed during moments of stress and anger into the most powerful creature to walk the Earth – the Hulk!

Doc Samson, a brilliant scientist whose body has also been augmented by gamma-radiation, attempts a daring procedure to permanently split Bruce Banner from the Hulk. The experiment is a success and a now hulk-free Banner marries his true love Betty Ross. But after a few months, Banner begins to deteriorate and in order to survive he is forced to merge once again with the Hulk.

After a number of adventures, Banner is permanently transformed into a more cunning and intelligent version of the Hulk and ends up working in Las Vegas as a mob enforcer named Joe Fixit. Whilst there, he begins a relationship with a woman named Marlo Chandler. After a while Bruce Banner manages to regain control of the Hulk, so that he now only turns into the monster at night, but remains human during the day.

Eventually, Banner decides to track down his estranged wife Betty, who believes that Bruce is dead. He makes his way to New York, unaware that he is being pursued by both Doc Samson and a mysterious hi-tech automobile...

WHAT THE HECK?!

IT BUGS ME THAT I'M THIS CLOSE TO CONNECTICUT, AND I HAVE TO CALL IT QUITS. BUT THE SUN'S GONNA BE *UP* IN A COUPLE MINUTES...

AND I *DON'T* WANT TO TAKE A CHANCE OF GETTING CAUGHT MIDAIR AGAIN WHILE CHANGING INTO BANNER.

LOOKS LIKE A FIREWORKS DISPLAY.

BUT THERE'S SOMETHING REALLY *HINKY* ABOUT IT.

IF *BANNER* TRIES TO LAND FROM A COUPLE THOUSAND FEET UP, THE LAST THING THAT'LL GO THROUGH HIS *MIND*...

...WILL BE HIS *FEET.*

WONDER WHAT'S *CAUSING* IT?

WONDER WHY I *CARE?*

HMMM...

EVERY TIME I'M INCLINED TO DISMISS THE IDEA THAT FATE GUIDES US...

SOMETHING SUCH AS *THIS* COMES ALONG.

WHEN, OF ALL THE PLACES IN THIS VAST CITY, I FIND MYSELF BY HAPPENSTANCE DRAWN TO A SINGLE BUILDING...

THAT *ALSO* ATTRACTS NONE OTHER THAN THE *HULK.*

MY FORMER PARTNER IN *CRIMES*...

...AND *HEROICS.*

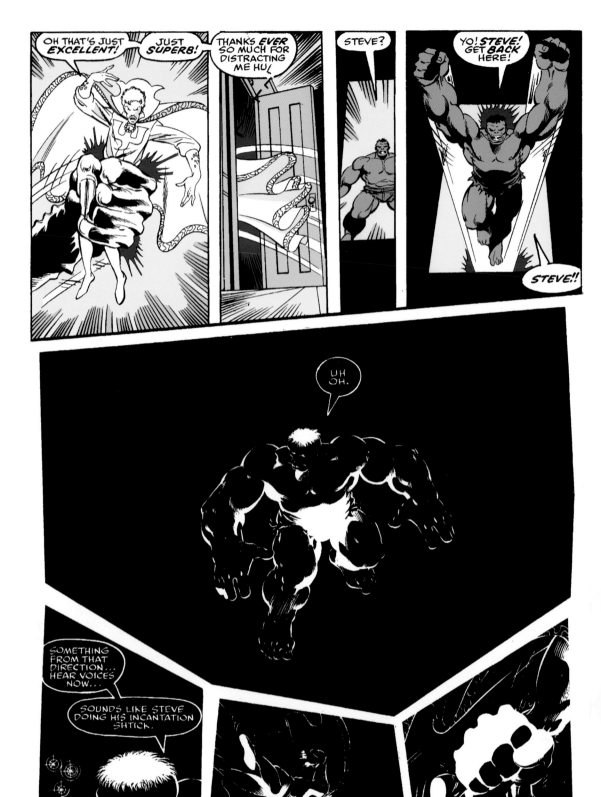

YOU'RE *ANCHORED* HERE, HULK. TAKE MY *WORD* ON THAT.

I HAVE A GREAT DEAL OF *EXPERIENCE* WITH ANCHORS.

SOMETHIN'S GRABBED ME ON THE OTHER SIDE...

...AND *WHATEVER* IT IS...

...IT'S *GOTTA* BE BETTER THAN *YOU!*

NYUUNNHHHH!

IF SOMEONE KNOCKS, I'M NOT HERE.

HUH!

WELL, *THAT* SURE FIGURES. I WONDERED WHO WAS STRONG ENOUGH TO TOSS *ME* AROUND LIKE A POKER CHIP.

THERE ARE INDEED A SELECT HANDFUL WHO FIT THAT CATEGORY...

...AND CERTAINLY NAMOR THE SUB-MARINER CAN BE NUMBERED *AMONG* THEM.

I SAW YOU ENTER THIS APARTMENT, CLEARLY ABOUT TO ENCOUNTER SOME SORT OF ELEMENTAL *FORCE.* IT PUT ME IN MIND OF OUR DAYS AS EARTH'S *DEFENDERS.*

YEAH, SWELL.

SO WHAT DO WE DO ABOUT CASPER THE FRIENDLY *MAGE* OVER THERE?

OVER *WHERE?*

THERE! RIGHT *THERE!*

HMMM, WHAT IS THAT SURFACE WORLD EXPRESSION? OH, YES...

WHAT ARE YOU *SMOKING,* HULK?

BUT HE'S *RIGHT HERE!* I CAN EVEN...

...TOUCH HIM?

STEVE! WAKEY *WAKEY!*

STEVE? OF *COURSE!* STEPHEN STRANGE IS IN THIS ROOM!

WELL, HE *WAS.*

I'VE HEARD OF SOMEONE SLIPPING THROUGH THE CRACKS, BUT THAT'S *RIDICULOUS.*

I FORGOT. ONLY *I* CAN SEE HIM WHEN HE'S IN THAT SPIRIT FORM OF HIS.

WHOLE *WORLD'S* GOING NUTS. HEY, NAMOR, I SAW A HEADLINE SAID YOU WERE *DEAD.*

AH, BUT THE PUBLIC HAS READ OF *YOUR* DEMISE, TOO. NOT ONLY THAT, BUT I SEEM TO RECALL DOCTOR STRANGE'S *FUNERAL.*

ALL OF US, MEN WHO ARE *ALIVE* WHEN, BY RIGHTS, WE SHOULD BE *DEAD.* DO YOU KNOW WHAT THAT MAKES US?

SURE, THE CHALLENGERS OF THE UNKNOWN.

NO. THREE VERY PROFICIENT *LIARS.*

WHAT DID YOU *SEE* WHILE YOU WERE *WITHIN?*

NOT SURE. EVERYTHING FELT DENSER, COMPRESSED... AND *REVERSED.* WEIRDEST THING I EVER SAW.

MAYBE I--

ARRHHHH!

HULK, YOU'RE IN PAIN! LET ME HELP--

NO! NOTHIN' *YOU* CAN DO.

I *KNOW* THIS... PARTICULAR PAIN.

IT'S A PAIN IN THE *BUTT...* CALLED...

...BRUCE BANNER.

BANNER. MY *APOLOGIES*... I WAS STARTLED BY THE *ABRUPTNESS* OF THE TRANSFORMATION. THERE WAS NO SHIFT IN THE HULK'S EMOTIONAL STATE, AND I WAS NOT EXPECT-ING...

YOU WOULDN'T *KNOW*, PRINCE NAMOR. WE SWITCH AT SUNRISE AND SUNSET NOW.

NICE *SUIT*, BY THE WAY.

GEORGIO ARMANI. SURFACE DWELLERS MAY HAVE *PATHETIC* BODIES, BUT THEY DRAPE THEM IN *QUALITY* CLOTHING.

ALTHOUGH *YOUR* FRAME SEEMS MORE *MUSCULAR* SINCE LAST WE MET.

THINK SO? I HADN'T *NOTICED*.

UHHHH... MIND FILLING ME IN ON WHAT JUST HAP-PENED?

AND...

WELL, IT SEEMS TO ME THE *SMART* THING TO DO IS GO TO DOCTOR STRANGE'S HOME AND WAIT FOR HIM THERE. DO YOU *AGREE*?

I SHALL HAVE TO MAKE SOME CALLS, REARRANGE MY SCHEDULE, BUT IT SEEMS *WORTHWHILE*.

I HAVE DECIDED TO BE MORE *SUBTLE* IN MY DEALINGS WITH THE SURFACE WORLD, YOU SEE. I ALLOW THE WORLD TO THINK ME *DEAD*...

WHILE GOING ABOUT MY BUSINESS WITH AN IDENTITY, WEARING THE *FINEST* SUITS, ENJOYING THE *BEST* THAT THE SURFACE WORLD HAS TO OFFER.

AN *EXCELLENT* PLAN, REALLY. PERHAPS THE *HULK* SHOULD TRY IT SOMETIME.

I'LL PASS THAT *ALONG*.

WHAT AN *ODD* BUSINESS.

THE NEXT THING I KNOW, A REFUGEE FROM "GHOST-BUSTERS" IS TRYING TO DRAG ME INTO A NETHER REALM I'VE NEVER *EXPERIENCED* BEFORE.

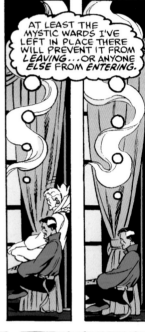

AT LEAST THE MYSTIC WARDS I'VE LEFT IN PLACE THERE WILL PREVENT IT FROM *LEAVING*... OR ANYONE ELSE FROM *ENTERING*.

FIRST I'M DRAWN TO A DISRUPTION IN TIME AND SPACE THAT SEEMED TO LOCALIZE IN THE APARTMENT OF WHAT *APPEARED* TO BE AN OLD WOMAN, JUDGING FROM THE FURNISHINGS...

AH. I *DIDN'T* IMAGINE IT. BRUCE BANNER, SOMETIMES KNOWN AS HULK...

...AND *NAMOR!* THIS IS OLD HOME WEEK.

YOU'RE SOUNDING SOMEWHAT MORE *COLLOQUIAL* THAN BEFORE, DOCTOR.

THINGS *CHANGE,* NAMOR. BRUCE, YOU MAY NOT WANT TO *HEAR* IT, BUT I *BELIEVE* YOUR ALTER EGO SAVED ME. WHY DON'T WE DIS-CUSS...

BEFORE WE DISCUSS *ANYTHING,* STEPHEN, IF I COULD JUST LIE *DOWN* FOR A WHILE, GET SOME REST?

BY ALL MEANS...UHM... BRUCE...THAT'S A *NASTY* SCAR YOU HAVE THERE. ON YOUR NECK.

WHAT? HMMM... HADN'T *NOTICED* IT BEFORE. ODD.

GOOD *GOING*, DOCTOR BANNER. ANNOUNCE YOU NEED REST, GO UPSTAIRS, LIE DOWN... AND STARE AT THE *CEILING* FOR A FEW HOURS.

THIS *INSOMNIA* IS STARTING TO BECOME *CHRONIC*. MAYBE THAT'S WHAT'S BEEN MAKING ME SO *IRRITABLE* LATELY.

AND MY *BACK* IS ITCHING. I'M STARTING TO FEEL THE SORE THAT DOCTOR STRANGE NOTICED.

WELL... NO NEED TO BOTHER *HIM* WITH IT.

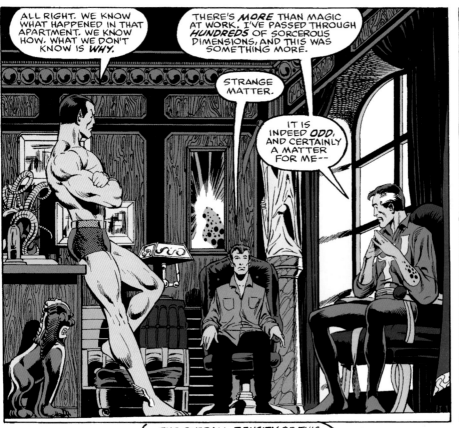

ALL RIGHT. WE KNOW WHAT HAPPENED IN THAT APARTMENT. WE KNOW HOW. WHAT WE DON'T KNOW IS *WHY*.

THERE'S *MORE* THAN MAGIC AT WORK. I'VE PASSED THROUGH *HUNDREDS* OF SORCEROUS DIMENSIONS, AND THIS WAS SOMETHING MORE.

STRANGE MATTER.

IT IS INDEED *ODD*, AND CERTAINLY A MATTER FOR ME--

NO, YOU DON'T *UNDERSTAND*. THE HEAVINESS THAT YOU AND NAMOR REFERRED TO...

...THE OVERALL *DENSITY* OF THIS "OTHER DIMENSION"... IT SOUNDS LIKE SOMETHING WE THEORIZED ABOUT BACK IN MY DAYS AT CAL-TECH, CALLED "STRANGE MATTER."

STRANGE MATTER IS INFINITELY MORE *DENSE* THAN SO-CALLED REAL MATTER. CONSERVATIVE THEORIES ARE THAT, IF IT EXISTS, IT COULD BE A VALUABLE *ENERGY* SOURCE.

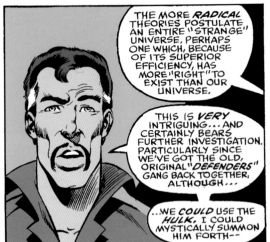

THE MORE *RADICAL* THEORIES POSTULATE AN ENTIRE "STRANGE" UNIVERSE, PERHAPS ONE WHICH, BECAUSE OF ITS SUPERIOR EFFICIENCY, HAS MORE "RIGHT" TO EXIST THAN OUR UNIVERSE.

THIS IS *VERY* INTRIGUING... AND CERTAINLY BEARS FURTHER INVESTIGATION, PARTICULARLY SINCE WE'VE GOT THE OLD, ORIGINAL "*DEFENDERS*" GANG BACK TOGETHER, ALTHOUGH...

...WE *COULD* USE THE *HULK*, I COULD MYSTICALLY SUMMON HIM FORTH--

I WOULDN'T *SUGGEST* IT. SUNLIGHT IS *ANATHEMA*, AND BESIDES, HE MIGHT NOT WANT TO *CO-OPERATE*.

COULD YOU CONVINCE HIM?

IF *ANYONE* COULD, DON'T WORRY, I CAN HANDLE HIM.

SUCH RESOLVE IN YOUR VOICE IS *REFRESHING*, BRUCE. I BELIEVE I CAN SET UP A "CONFERENCE CALL."

IT'S FORTUNATE THE SILVER SURFER ISN'T HERE. AS I RECALL, IF THE FOUR OF US EVER *REUNITED*, IT WOULD RESULT IN THE EARTH'S *DESTRUCTION*.

YOU KNOW, DOCTOR, I MUST *ADMIT* I ALWAYS FOUND THAT A BIT HARD TO SWALLOW.

SO DID *I*. THAT'S WHY I DID FURTHER INVESTI-GATION AFTER WE DISBANDED.

FOUND OUT IT WAS ALL A COSMIC *HOAX*. WE CAN REUNITE ANY TIME WE WANT.

WHAT?! WHY DIDN'T YOU *SAY* SOMETHING *MONTHS* AGO?

BECAUSE, FRANKLY, THE PEACE AND QUIET AROUND HERE WAS A WELCOME *CHANGE*. NOW PLEASE, I MUST CONCENTRATE...

...AS THE EYE OF AGOMOTTO OPENS UP A PATHWAY...

"...TO THE DARK SIDE OF A MAN'S MIND."

YEAH? AND WHADDA*YOU* WANT?

WE NEED TO *TALK*, HULK. YOUR HELP IS NEEDED BY THE DEFENDERS.

AW, THAT'S *GREAT!* NOW WE'RE BRINGING *THAT* LAME-O TEAM BACK? WHO'S NEXT? THE BOY COMMANDOS?

I DON'T LIKE THIS *EITHER*, HULK, BUT DOCTOR STRANGE WANTS YOU...*US*...AS ALLIES.

I *DID* MY BIT. I HELPED STEVE *ONCE* TODAY. AND CONSIDERING *HE'S* THE QUACK WHO DUMPED ME IN THE MIDDLE OF DIMENSIONAL NOWHERE A WHILE AGO, THAT WAS PRETTY *NICE* OF ME.

BUT I FIGURED I OWED HIM *SOMETHING* FOR ALL THE TIMES HE WAS DECENT TO ME.

THAT'S *EXCELLENT*, HULK! REALIZING THAT SOMETIMES YOU HAVE OBLIGATIONS *BEYOND* MONETARY GAIN...THAT'S A BIG *STEP* FOR YOU.

JUST AS WE NOW HAVE AN OBLIGATION TO STAY AND INVESTIGATE WHATEVER THAT SINISTER FORCE *IS*, THAT STRANGE MATTER WORLD.

THE HECK WE DO! YOU TALK TO ME ABOUT OBLIGATIONS? WHAT ABOUT AN OBLIGATION TO *BETTY*, HUH?

REMEMBER HER? OUR...

YOUR WIFE, WHAT ABOUT *HER*?

AREN'T YOU OBLIGED TO *HER*?

WE'LL *GET* TO HER, BUT THE *IMPORTANT* THING IS--

HOLD IT. BACK UP.

STEVE AND FISH FACE, *THEY* CAN PLAY HERO. *LOTS* OF PEOPLE CAN PLAY HERO. BUT ONLY *YOU* CAN GO TO YOUR WIFE.

KNOW WHAT *I* THINK? I THINK YOU'RE *AFRAID* TO FIND HER. AFRAID OF *WHAT* YOU'LL FIND.

THAT'S RIDICULOUS.

YEAH? AND YOU'VE SURE TAKEN YOUR OWN SWEET *TIME* FINDING HER. SO WHAT'RE YOU *AFRAID* OF? MAYBE THAT SHE WON'T *LOVE* YOU ANYMORE? MAYBE THAT SHE LOVES *ME* NOW INSTEAD?

SHUT UP!

SHE AND I *DID* GET PRETTY *CHUMMY* ON THOSE CLIFFS...

I SAID *SHUT* YOUR FILTHY *YAP!* I'M NOT AFRAID OF--

EH?

WHAT'S *THIS* THING? NEVER *SAW* IT BEFORE.

WHATEVER IT IS, IT'S BLOCKING OUR *PATH.*

MAYBE IT'S A MENTAL BLOCK.

OH, YOU'RE A *RIOT,* HULK. SO... OPEN IT.

NO WAY.

AREN'T YOU *CURIOUS?*

NOT *THAT* CURIOUS. YOU'RE SO BRAVE, *YOU* OPEN IT.

I HAVEN'T THE STRENGTH.

DOESN'T TAKE STRENGTH, JUST *GUTS.* BUT YOU DON'T HAVE *EITHER.*

AND YOU HAVE *BOTH,* EH? BUT *YOU* WON'T OPEN IT. IN MY BOOK, THAT MAKES YOU A COWARD.

WHAT?

A COWARD, A GUTLESS, CRAVEN WIMP.

WHAT'VE YOU GOT, A *DEATH* WISH?!

WE'VE *BEEN* THROUGH THAT, HULK. YOU, WITH ALL YOUR BLUSTER, WOULDN'T *DARE* HURT ME. YOU'RE AFRAID OF WHAT MIGHT *HAPPEN.* YOU *NEED* ME.

NEXT: SERIOUS BREAKAGE

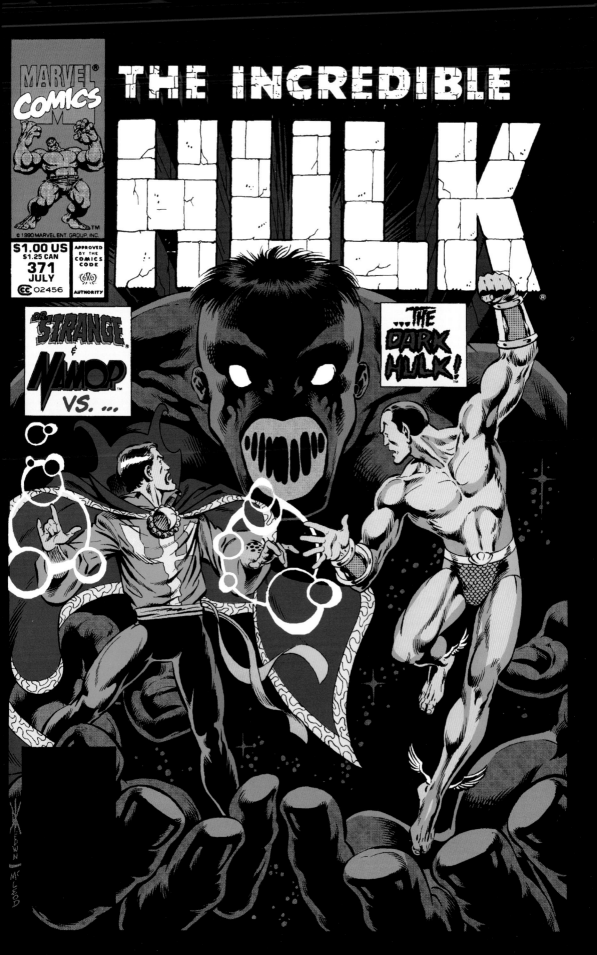

BY THE POWER OF DORMAMMU AND MEPHISTO'S FIENDISH *EYES*...

LET THIS DEBRIS HURT *NO* PEOPLE...

...BUT INSTEAD REFORM INTO MY WINDOW!

EFFECTIVE, BUT IT DOESN'T *REMOTELY* RHYME.

EVERYONE'S A CRITIC. I'M A *DOCTOR*, NOT A POET.

ANNE...

I THINK WE'LL BE ABLE TO REMEMBER THIS *WITHOUT* A PICTURE.

ANNE? WAKE *UP*, SWEETHEART...

"...NO MATTER WHAT IT TAKES,"

I MUST WAIT UNTIL THE SUN SETS ...FOR THEN HIS BODY WILL BE AT ITS GREATEST STRENGTH, AND I CAN...

WHAT'S THAT... IN MY HEAD? OH, OF COURSE... THE PATHETIC HUMAN HALF OF THIS COMBINATION. I HEAR IT NATTERING ABOUT.

YOU IN THERE? QUIET! I MUST CONCENTRATE ON MY BUSINESS.

WHATEVER YOU ARE-- I DON'T KNOW HOW YOU MANAGED TO TAKE OVER THE HULK'S PSYCHE...

...BUT I'M ORDERING YOU OUT! THIS MENTAL PLANE IS MINE! GET OUT OF HERE!

YOU FOOL. NOT ONLY AM I HERE ON THIS "MENTAL PLANE," AS YOU CALL IT...

...BUT I'VE USURPED YOUR PHYSICAL PRESENCE AS WELL.

AND THERE IS NOTHING YOU CAN DO TO STOP IT.

THE DEVIL THERE ISN'T!!

RELEASE MY MIND AND BODY... NOW!

INTERESTING. THE POWER OF YOUR MIND MAKES UP FOR SOME OF YOUR LACK OF PHYSICAL PROWESS...

SOME...BUT *NOT* ENOUGH.

WHAT...*ARE* YOU?

AS YOU THEORIZED... A DENIZEN OF A "STRANGE UNIVERSE" OF GREATER MOLECULAR DENSITY.

I AM, IN FACT, THE *SORCERER SUPREME* OF THAT UNIVERSE, MUCH AS YOUR *DOCTOR STRANGE* IS HERE... EXCEPT I HAVE HELD THAT POSITION FOR *MILLENNIA*.

BUT... BUT THEN WHAT ARE YOU DOING *HERE*? DON'T YOU HAVE *ENOUGH* TO DO, WATCHING OVER YOUR *OWN* UNIVERSE?

AH, BUT THAT'S THE *PROBLEM*. WATCHING OVER ALL OF THEM... BECAME A BURDEN, SO I OBLITERATED THEM, MAKING THEM *EASIER* TO CARE FOR. EXCEPT...NOW I'M QUITE, QUITE LONELY, SO I NEED *NEW* CHALLENGES.

THE BODY OF THE OLD WOMAN CRUSHED *IMMEDIATELY* UPON ENTERING MY REALM... BUT *THIS* BODY IS SUPPORTING THE STRAINS OF MY NATURE QUITE W--

UNNHH!

IT SEEMS MY *PHYSICAL* ASPECT IS UNDER *ATTACK*. I'LL HAVE TO DEVOTE FULL CONCENTRATION TO THAT...

BUT IN THE MEANTIME, I THINK I'D BEST KEEP YOU *OUT* OF TROUBLE... UNTIL I DECIDE WHETHER I CAN SAFELY ELIMINATE YOU OR *NOT*.

YOU'RE *INSANE*!

AN *ODD* CRITICISM, CONSIDERING THE *SOURCE*.

BACK OUTSIDE THE ASTRAL PLANE...

SO...

YOU THOUGHT TO *DESTROY* ME WHILE MY ATTENTION WAS *ELSEWHERE,* EH?

WHERE YOUR ATTENTION IS IS OF *LITTLE* CONSEQUENCE TO ME.

WHAT CONCERNS ME IS WHERE YOUR *MIND* IS... NAMELY IN THE BODY OF ANOTHER. YOU WILL RETURN THAT *BODY* TO THE HOME OF DOCTOR STRANGE, AND THE *MIND* TO ITS ORIGINAL OWNER...

OR I SHALL BE *FORCED* TO RESORT TO...

...FISTICUFFS.

WHAÁAM

NYUUUUNNNHHH...

GOT TO... MAKE IT *THROUGH*...

WHILE HE'S...*DIS-TRACTED*...

ARRHHHH...

ARRHHHH...

WHOEVER... *WHAT*EVER YOU ARE...

YOU'RE ONLY MAKING IT...

...*HARDER* ON YOURSELF.

YOU'RE *BOASTFUL*, LITTLE MAN, I'LL GIVE YOU *THAT*.

BUT YOU SHOULD NOT ISSUE THREATS THAT YOU DO NOT HAVE THE *POWER* TO BACK UP.

HUNK

I SHALL *REMEMBER* THAT SAGE PIECE OF ADVICE...

K-RUNK

SHOULD MY POWER EVER BE *LACKING*...

A HAPPENSTANCE I *SERIOUSLY* DOUBT!

HAH! I'VE DONE IT!

ALL THAT YOU HAVE DONE IS HASTEN YOUR END.

EH!

THE CRIMSON BANDS OF CYTORRAK WILL HOLD YOU, FOR AS LONG AS IT TAKES...

...WHILE I RID THE WORLD OF YOUR PERNICIOUS PRESENCE.

HE'S STOPPED TALKING, STOPPED CHORTLING. SOMETHING MUST HAVE MENTALLY HAMMER-LOCKED HIM IN THE REAL WORLD.

AND IT'S ENOUGH TO DISTRACT HIM... SO THAT I CAN BE FREE.

EXCEPT... I HAVE NO IDEA WHERE TO GO.

AN EFFECTIVE TRAP... WITHIN THE BOUNDS OF *YOUR* UNIVERSE, MAGICIAN.

A PITY FOR YOU...

THAT *I* AM NOT GOVERNED BY *YOUR* LAWS!

MY UNIVERSE IS *INFINITELY* SUPERIOR TO YOURS, MAGE. MORE *EFFICIENT*... MORE *POWERFUL*, RIGHT DOWN TO ITS MOLECULAR BONDS.

MINE HAS THE RIGHT TO *EXIST*... TO *SUPPLANT* YOURS.

JUST AS *I* SHALL SUPPLANT *YOU!*

PERHAPS.

BUT *WHICH* OF US...

...WILL YOU SUP-PLANT?

KRONK

YOU... YOU *SHIELDED* ME... WITH YOUR BODY! HOW... HOW...

EXTRA FIBER IN MY DIET.

YOU'RE TOO MUCH OF A *HINDRANCE*, HUMAN! SO TELL ME...

HOW DO YOU WISH TO *DIE*?

OF OLD AGE!

AND YOU DON'T FOOL *ME!* YOU HAVEN'T THE *STRENGTH* TO OVERCOME THE FORCE OF *MY* PERSONALITY.

YOU *DELUDE* YOURSELF, *BANNER*. BUT *PRETEND* YOU HAVE THE STRENGTH TO *RESIST* ME, IF THAT DELUSION PROVES COMFORT--

ARRRGHHH!

YOU SHOULD NEVER CONVERSE WITH *ONE* FOE WHILE *ANOTHER* IS WAITING FOR YOU!

NAMOR! FALL *BACK!*

NAMOR RUNS FROM NO MAN!

THAT'S OKAY, BECAUSE THAT'S *NO MAN.* NOW COME ON...

BEFORE INJURIES ARE SUSTAINED THAT ARE *BEYOND* MY POWER TO REPAIR.

AND WE'RE JUST SUPPOSED TO LEAVE HIM, IS *THAT* IT?

NO, HE'LL BE COMING *AFTER* US. I USED THE EYE TO PLANT AN IRRESISTIBLE SUGGESTION. AND HE WON'T REALIZE THE SOURCE, UNTIL IT'S TOO LATE.

M...

WOOMF

AND COME THE MORNING...

YOU LOOK FIT TODAY, BRUCE,... AS DOES THE *ARCH.* NAMOR IS USING HIS CONSIDERABLE RESOURCES TO *RECONSTRUCT* IT. I, MEANTIME, HAVE CREATED WARDS OVER ALL CROSSING POINTS BETWEEN THE "STRANGE" UNIVERSE AND OUR OWN.

THAT'S GOOD TO HEAR.

DEAR HEAVEN, BRUCE, THAT SCAR RUNS ALL THE WAY DOWN YOUR *BACK* NOW! PERHAPS I'D BETTER--

--NOT *WORRY* ABOUT IT. IT'S *MY* PROBLEM. SPEAKING OF PROBLEMS,...DID YOU MANAGE TO FIND WHERE IN DARIEN, CONNECTI-CUT BETTY IS?

SHE'S AT 321 MAPLE ST.

EXCELLENT! YOUR MYSTIC EYE TOLD YOU?

NO, I MADE A FEW CALLS, FOUND HER OBSTETRICIAN. HE FORWARDED HER MEDICAL RECORDS THERE. WE DOCTORS STICK TOGETHER.

BRUCE... THERE'S NO *GOOD* WAY TO SAY IT. BETTY... HAD A *MISCARRIAGE.*

BRUCE... IF THERE'S ANYTHING I CAN--

NO, IT'S... IT'S FINE.

IT'S *BETTER* THIS WAY.

HE PROBABLY WOULD HAVE BEEN A FREAK. LIKE HIS *FATHER.*

BRUCE...I THINK PER-HAPS YOU SHOULD STAY *HERE* A DAY OR TWO....JUST TO GET OVER THE NEWS.

I'M *FINE.* NOW IF YOU'LL EXCUSE ME...

"I HAVE A *TRAIN* TO CATCH."

IT SHOULD BE THE NEXT BLOCK.

WHAT WILL I *SAY* TO HER? "HI, HONEY, SORRY I'VE BEEN DEAD ALL THIS TIME?" THAT HARDLY...

HMMM. THIS *CAN'T* BE RIGHT. 321 MAPLE IS A CONVENT.

NOW WHY IN THE *WORLD* WOULD SHE BE LIVING IN A--

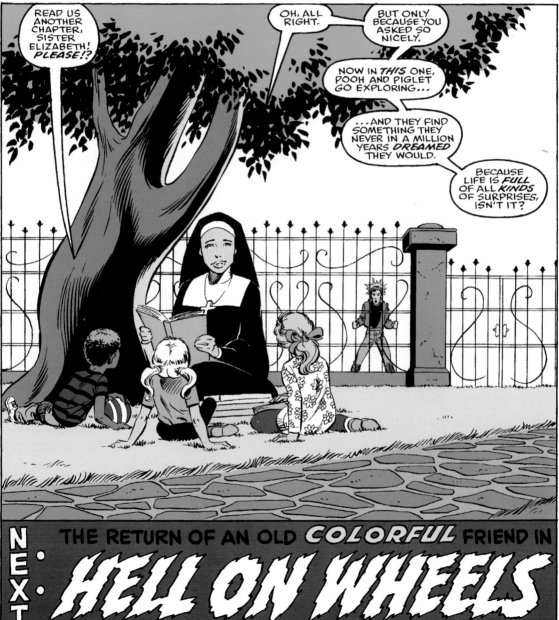

READ US ANOTHER CHAPTER, SISTER ELIZABETH! *PLEASE!?*

OH, ALL RIGHT.

BUT ONLY BECAUSE YOU ASKED SO NICELY.

NOW IN *THIS* ONE, POOH AND PIGLET GO EXPLORING...

...AND THEY FIND SOMETHING THEY NEVER IN A MILLION YEARS *DREAMED* THEY WOULD.

BECAUSE LIFE IS *FULL* OF ALL *KINDS* OF SURPRISES, ISN'T IT?

NEXT: THE RETURN OF AN OLD *COLORFUL* FRIEND IN

HELL ON WHEELS

KNOK
KNOK

YES?

HELLO, SISTER, I'M HERE TO SEE *BETTY BANNER.* IT'S VERY, *VERY,* IMPORTANT.

SISTER ELIZABETH IS A POSTULANT AT THIS CONVENT, AND HAS MADE IT QUITE CLEAR SHE WISHES TO SEE *NO ONE.*

BUT YOU SEE, I'M--

OH, I *KNOW* WHO YOU ARE. THE LATEST OF A HUNDRED REPORTERS WITH SOME NEW EXCUSE TO SEE HER. ELIZABETH BANNER HAS BEEN THROUGH *ENOUGH.*

NOW PLEASE *LEAVE* BEFORE I CALL THE AUTHORITIES.

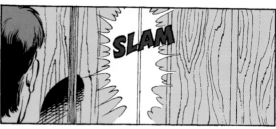

SLAM

UNH...

THEY CAN REFUSE TO SEE ME, HANG *UP* ON ME ¿UNH¿

BUT THEY *CAN'T* KEEP ME *OUT.*

RIIP

OH, GREAT.

DOCTOR STRANGE SAID THERE'S A *SCAR* ON MY BACK. I HOPE IT'S NOT *NOTICE-ABLE.*

I DON'T THINK THAT MAN'S SUPPOSED TO BE HERE. I'M TELLING.

I HAVE SIMPLY **GOT** TO GET A NEW WATCH.

THE SISTERS ARE GOING TO BE **MOST** UPSET OVER MY TARDI-NESS. THEY'RE SO **PUNCTUAL** ABOUT TAKING CONFESSION.

HMMM...IF I BREAK THE SPEED LIMIT ON A HOLY MISSION, IS THAT--

EH?

LOOK OUT!!

SSSCCRREEE

SHOOOOM

KRUNK

A CHAPEL OF SOME KIND.

THIS IS RIDICULOUS. SHE COULD BE **ANYWHERE** IN THE CONVENT, OR--

UH-OH.

SOMEONE'S COMING IN THE FAR ENTRANCE.

WOULDN'T DO TO BE DISCOVERED ....SO...

OH, WONDER-FUL. I'M HIDING IN A CONFES-SIONAL. HAVE TO GET **OUT** OF--

BLESS ME, FATHER....

...FOR I HAVE SINNED.

IT HAS BEEN A WEEK SINCE MY LAST CONFESSION. I'VE WORKED HARD, TAUGHT THE DAY SCHOOL, AND PRAYED FOR *GUIDANCE*.

I'VE HAD SUCH A...A *DIFFICULT* LIFE, FATHER. LOSING MY MOTHER, BEING SENT TO BOARDING SCHOOL, RETURNING TO LIVE WITH A FATHER WHO WAS A *STRANGER* TO ME.

MY WHOLE LIFE HAS BEEN SO UNBALANCED. I'VE SPENT IT SEEKING CONSTANCY AND STEADINESS...AND NEVER *FOUND* IT.

INSTEAD OF *FINDING*, I'M ALWAYS *LOSING*. I'VE LOVED THREE MEN AND LOST THEM *ALL*. LOST MY *BABY*. LOST... MY VERY *IDENTITY*.

I'M RAMBLING. I'M SORRY. IT'S JUST THAT...

I'VE RICOCHETED FROM IDENTITY TO IDENTITY. STUDENT, AIR FORCE BRAT, DAUGHTER, WIFE, EX-WIFE, MADWOMAN... AND I...

...I LOST BETTY ROSS SOMEWHERE.

THEY *KILLED* BETTY, FATHER. THE IDENTITIES, AND THE DEATHS, AND... AND THE *MONSTERS*. ALL THE MONSTERS KILLED HER.

AND THEN, IN THE HOSPITAL AFTER I LOST MY BABY, THE NUNS WERE SO *GOOD* TO ME. AND THE PICTURE OF JESUS WAS HANGING IN MY HOSPITAL ROOM, AND I THOUGHT, "OF COURSE."

"*THAT'S* WHAT I'VE NEEDED ALL MY LIFE."

"THE CHURCH I'VE *IGNORED* FOR SO MANY YEARS. I NEED LOVE OF *SPIRIT* RATHER THAN *FLESH*."

"I NEED *PEACE*. NO MORE HOPELESS LOVE. NO MORE MONSTERS. JUST SWEET, BLESSED *PEACE*."

MY TIME IN THE CONVENT HAS BEEN EVERY-THING I *HOPED* FOR. AFTER ALL THE RUNNING AND HORROR, CONFUSION AND UNCERTAINTY... THERE IS *PEACE* HERE.

DEVOTION AND THANKFULNESS. NO UNCERTAINTY OR MONSTERS.

NO BRUCE BANNER.

I'M...

I'M *HAPPY* FOR YOU...

...MY *CHILD*...

FATHER...THERE'S *MORE* I HAVE TO SAY. YOU SEE--

YOU LOOK OVER *THERE*, AND I'LL TRY IN *HERE*!

GOOD HEAVENS, WHAT'S THE *RUCKUS* OUT HERE?

SISTER! HAVE YOU *SEEN* HIM?

SEEN *WHO*?

LITTLE RACHEL SAID SHE SAW A MAN CLIMBING OVER THE FENCE...HE'S ON THE *GROUNDS* SOMEWHERE. WE'VE CALLED THE POLICE, BUT IT WILL TAKE THEM SOME TIME TO GET HERE.

MOST OF THEM ARE PURSUING SOME *INSANE* DRIVER WHO GOT FATHER LOWRY INTO AN ACCIDENT.

WHAT? BUT...BUT I WAS JUST GIVING *CONFESSION* TO FATHER LOWRY!

I WAS IN THE MIDDLE OF--

--OF--

HE'S *GONE*!

SHE *HATES* ME.

HOW CAN I *BLAME* HER... AFTER EVERYTHING I'VE *DONE* TO HER.

I'VE INVADED *EVERY* ASPECT OF HER--HER *MIND,* HER *BODY,* PUT HER THROUGH EVERY *IMAGINABLE* TORTURE. *I* HAVE...

ALTHOUGH I'VE HAD SOME *HELP...* HAVEN'T I?

IT ALL STARTED SO *INNOCENTLY,* LORD... SHE WAS THE FIRST GIRL I EVER LOOKED AT WHO MADE ME *SHAKE* INSIDE.

AND WHAT I DID TO HER... WHAT I *DID*...

IT WOULD BE THE HEIGHT OF *SELFISHNESS* TO TRY AND BRING HER *BACK* TO ME.

BUT SHE'S MARRIED TO ME... A NUN CAN'T BE MARRIED. SHE'S LIVING A *LIE.*

EXCEPT... I'M OFFICIALLY *DEAD.* SO WE'RE PROBABLY *NOT* MARRIED. AND SHE'S HAPPY... AND AT PEACE...

"HOW CAN I *ROB* HER OF THAT?"

MOTHER SUPERIOR?

WHY... ELIZABETH ...WHATEVER IS *WRONG?*

WHY HAVE YOU CHANGED OUT OF--?

I'M *LEAVING* THE CONVENT, MOTHER SUPERIOR.

IT'S WHAT I WAS STARTING TO TELL FATHER LOWRY...OR *THOUGHT* I WAS.

HAS SOMETHING HERE MADE YOU *UN-HAPPY,* ELIZABETH?

OH, NO, YOU'VE ALL BEEN *WONDER-FUL,* THAT'S THE *POINT.*

I'VE FOUND SUCH *PEACE* HERE, BUT...I'M *NOT* HAPPY. IT'S *BRUCE.*

I HEARD THE REPORTS, WITH BRUCE OR THE HULK SEEN *HERE* OR *THERE.* I DON'T GIVE IT ANY *CREDENCE,* ANY MORE THAN PRISCILLA PRESLEY GETS EXCITED WHEN ELVIS IS "SEEN" IN AN A&P.

BUT I CAN'T STOP HOPING AND PRAYING... CAN'T STOP *LOVING* HIM ...EVEN THOUGH IT'S *HOPELESS,* BECAUSE HE'S *GONE.* EVEN SOME *STRANGER* IN A *CONFESSION-AL* REMINDED ME OF HIM.

I CAN'T LOVE JESUS WITH ALL MY HEART IF MY HEART IS, FIRST AND FOREMOST, BOUND TO SOMEONE *ELSE.* AND I'VE COME TO REALIZE THAT I DON'T *WANT* TO.

YOU KNOW, WHEN I WAS A TEACHER AT THE BOARD-ING SCHOOL THAT YOUNG BETTY ROSS WAS SENT TO...

I SAW A *FIRE* IN HER EYES, A FLAME. I *LIKED* THAT.

NOW, WHEN OUR PATHS CROSSED YEARS LATER, I SAW THAT FIRE WAS *GONE.*

FRANKLY, ELIZABETH, I *WASN'T* SURE IF THE CHURCH WAS THE *ANSWER* FOR YOU, BUT I WAS WILLING TO GIVE YOU THE *CHANCE.* I KNEW, GIVEN TIME, YOU'D FIND THE *ANSWER.*

BUT I DON'T KNOW IF I *HAVE* YET, MOTHER SUPERIOR.

PERHAPS, BUT YOU'VE FOUND THAT THE ANSWER DOESN'T LIE *HERE...* BUT IN *YOU.*

"AND I THINK I SEE, ELIZABETH, IF NOT A *FIRE*...AT LEAST A *SPARK*."

IT'S CLEAR, THEN. I CAN'T JUST...

EH?

BETTY?

BUT...BUT SHE'S NOT WEARING THE *HABIT?* WHAT'S GOING--

BETTY!!

VROOOM

TELEPHONE

YES, IS BETTY ROSS BANNER THERE?

I AM AFRAID THAT, FOR PERSONAL REASONS, ELIZABETH HAS *LEFT* THE ORDER. SO IF YOU'RE ANOTHER JOURNALIST...

NO! THIS IS, UH...

ACE CABS. I'M DA *DISPATCHUH*. ONE OF OUR GUYS, HE PICKED HER UP, BUT WE GOT NO RECORD OF DA DESTINATION. WE NEED IT FOR ANOTHUH PICK-UP.

I BELIEVE HER DESTINATION IS THE *AMTRAK* STATION. BUT DON'T YOUR CABS HAVE *RADIOS* TO--

HELLO?

I'VE BEEN A *FOOL* ALL THIS TIME. I SHOULD'VE DEVOTED *ALL* MY ENERGY TO FINDING HER.

I'VE BEEN *AFRAID.* AFRAID TO SUBJECT HER TO LIFE WITH *ME* AGAIN.

BUT WE'LL WORK IT OUT. SOMEHOW.

ALL THAT MATTERS IS THAT WE'RE *TOGETHER.*

AMTRAK
NEXT RIGHT

CHOOOM

WHAT?!

KRAKAAM

WHERE'S THE NEXT TRAIN TO?

NEW YORK. FROM THERE YOU CAN TRANSFER JUST ABOUT ANYWHERE.

TICKETS

FORM LINE HERE

THAT SOUNDS *FINE.*

AND IT SO HAPPENS IT LEAVES IN FIVE MINUTES, PRETTY LADY. THIS IS YOUR *LUCKY* DAY.

BETTY! *BETTY,* *WAIT!*

SHE CAN'T *HEAR* ME! THAT INSANE *CAR* IS DROWNING ME OUT! BETTY!

NO!

WHO *ARE* YOU?! WHY ARE YOU *DOING* THIS?!

MOUNT, THIS IS *PROMETHEUS.* TARGET'S IN SIGHT.

OOOOFF!

HE SPRAYED *OIL* ON THE STREET TO TRIP ME UP! WHO *IS* THAT?

SHOOOMF

OH NO!

I'VE *GOT* HIM, MOUNT, AND SINCE IT'S ONLY MID-AFTERNOON, I DON'T HAVE TO WORRY ABOUT THE *HULK* POKING HIS GRAY FACE INTO THIS. ALL OF WHICH MEANS...

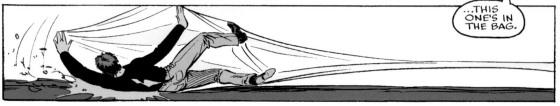

...THIS ONE'S IN THE BAG.

NO! I'VE PUT UP WITH *EVERYTHING!* GONE *THROUGH* EVERYTHING... BUT NOT *THIS* TOO!

I WON'T LOSE HER AGAIN! *ANYTHING* BUT *THAT!*

ANYTHING! ANYTHING!!

KRRIIIP

SON OF A...

SKREEE

MOUNT, HE BROKE OUT OF THE BAG. I DON'T LIKE THAT AT *ALL.*

AND HE LOOKS *REALLY* HACKED OFF. LIKE HE'S READY TO JUMP OUT OF HIS *SKIN.*

I DON'T KNOW WHO YOU ARE, AND I DON'T *CARE!*

I'M *SICK* OF BEING KICKED AND SHOVED AROUND AND TREATED LIKE *DIRT!*

I'VE *HAD* IT! I WANT *BETTY!*

AND *YOU* WON'T STOP ME! SO GET *OUT* OF MY WAY!

YOU HEAR?! *OUT! OUT!!*

OUUWWWW

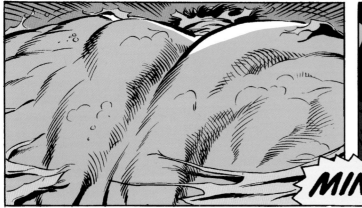

THE COMBO OF THE FLAME AND PULSE BLASTS SEEMS TO HAVE *SOFTENED* HIM SOMEWHAT, MOUNT.

CAR THOUGHT IT *HURT* HULK.

BUT HULK *CAN'T* HURT CAR.

BECAUSE CAR IS ONLY STUPID *MACHINE!*

CAN'T *BLEED*. JUST *BREAK*.

CAN'T *DIE*. JUST *STOP*.

BUT IF STINKING *HUMAN* IS *INSIDE* CAR, THE HUMAN *CAN* BE HURT. HE CAN *BLEED* AND *DIE*.

RAKAAM

AND HULK WILL MAKE *SURE* HE DOES!

SSS

SSS

EH?

CAN'T *SEE* ME, HUH, HULK? DON'T WORRY...

BECAUSE I'VE GOT *YOU*, BABE.

CHAK

CHAK

CHAK

WHAT *IS* THIS?

OOOFF!

ZZZZZZTTTT

NO ONE...TAKES HULK...WHERE HULK DOESN'T *WANT* TO GO...

SNAP

KRAK

KRAK

GOING FOR DEEP FREEZE.

BLIIIIZZZZ

STUPID CAR IS GONE.

GOOD. MADE HULK *ANGRY.*

AND THERE WAS...SOME-THING *ELSE...*

HARD TO REMEMBER. LIKE...SOMEONE ELSE...

BUT I'M NOT... I MEAN, *HULK* ISN'T...

HULK...

THE GREEN HULK...BUT WHAT ABOUT THE *GRAY,* AND...

BETTY?

BETTY! WAIT!

STOP THE *TRAIN!*

CHUK CHUK

CHUK

STOP! BETTY *WAIT!*

COME BACK!!

CHUK CHUK

CHUK

CHUK

CHUK

CHUK

CHUK

NOT AGAIN... NOT AGAIN...

GET ANGRY...COME *ON*...GET ANGRY, AND THE HULK CAN...

OH, LORD...IS *THIS* WHAT I'VE COME TO? *WISH-ING* FOR THE HULK?

PLEASE...*DON'T* LET THIS HAPPEN... PLEASE...

GIVE ME A *SHRED* OF HAPPINESS...

DON'T TAKE HER AWAY...

PLEASE...

please...

EVERYTHING WAS GOING *GREAT!* I WAS BUILDING MY OWN REP, BEATING ALL THE LOSERS WHO THOUGHT I WAS EASY PICKINGS! THE THING, THE ABOMINATION, THE BLOB-- *ALL* OF 'EM!

I'D ALMOST MADE THE WORLD *FORGET* I USED TO HAVE THE BRAINS AND SKIN COLORING OF AN *AVOCADO!*

AND THEN *YOU* HAD TO SHOW UP! WITH YOUR MUSCLES AND YOUR CLICHE-RIDDEN "HULK SMASH" SHTICK! BUG *OFF*, GREENIE! BANNER AND I WERE DOING FINE *WITHOUT* YA!

HULK *HATES* PUNY BANNER!

AND HULK HATES STUPID *DOOR!*

AND *MOST* OF ALL...

HULK HATES *YOU!!*

LOOK! *BEHIND* YA! AIN'T THAT *LOU FERRIGNO?!*

WHAT? WHO?

SLAM

CHUNK

BRUCE, BETTY LOU--

YOU FIRST.

BRUCE, IT'S...IT'S A *MIRACLE!*

WELL, IF ANYONE WAS EVER ENTITLED TO A MIRACLE, IT'S *US.*

HOLD IT! DON'T MOVE!

WE WANT TO TALK TO YOU PEOPLE!

I WOULD CONSIDER THAT A CONVERSATION WITH *LITTLE* SOCIAL VALUE.

LET'S GO!

DO YOU THINK THEY'RE UPSET BECAUSE I JUMPED OFF A MOVING TRAIN?

WELL, IT CERTAINLY DIDN'T *ENDEAR* YOU TO THEM.

HOLD IT, PEOPLE! I'M *NOT* KIDDING!

SOMEHOW I SUSPECTED THAT.

ELSEWHERE...

THERE HE GOES!!

JONES WENT *THAT* WAY!!

SPLIISH

GROWF
GROOWF
RAWRR

JONES! YOU *WON'T* GET AWAY!

JONES!

SNAP

GROWF

I *HATE* OVER-AGGRESSIVE FANS.

WHAT THE BLAZES WENT *ON* HERE?! I THOUGHT THIS KIND OF STUFF ONLY HAPPENED IN NEW YORK!

BEATS THE HECK OUTTA *ME.*

WELL, *SOMETHING* SURE BEAT THE HECK OUTTA *SOMETHING!*

MOVE ALONG, NOTHING TO SEE HERE.

I'LL TELL YOU IN *ONE* WORD WHAT HAPPENED HERE:

COMMIES.

GIVE IT A *REST*, PHIL.

WELL, I *STILL* DON'T TRUST 'EM.

HEY, WHO'S IN *THAT* CAR?

AW, GREAT. JUST GREAT. *FEDS.*

HOW DO *YOU* KNOW?

'CAUSE ALL THEIR UNMARKED CARS LOOK THE SAME,

AND THEY'RE ALWAYS TAKING CHARGE, THE FEDS ARE.

FBI. *WE'RE* TAKING CHARGE HERE.

YEAH? WHAT MAKES IT *YOUR* BUSINESS, FROSTY?

POSSIBLE IN-VOLVEMENT OF THE *HULK*, MISTER.

HULK, HUH? WELL, HE'LL SURE BE SCARED OF *YOU.*

SERGEANT, THIS IS *SERIOUS* BUSINESS.

I'LL TRY TO STOP *LAUGHING* AT YOU, THEN. TOUGH AS THAT MAY B–

SARGE!

GET A LOAD OF *THIS.*

WEIRDEST STIFF I EVER *SAW.*

UH-OH.

YES, I SEE THEM, TOO. BUT WE *CAN'T* GO BACK THE WAY WE CAME.

SO KEEP YOUR HEAD DOWN AND PRAY.

FORTUNATELY, WE'VE HAD PRACTICE AT THAT LATELY.

IT'S *NOT* A DEAD BODY. IT'S DEAD *SKIN*.

SHED LIKE A SNAKE'S. AS IF THE BODY HAD *OUTGROWN* IT.

BINGO.

THE FACE IS A POSITIVE I.D, TOO. BRUCE BANNER.

WE'RE TALKING A VARIATION ON THE CLASSIC HULK/BANNER CHANGE SCENARIO.

BINGO AGAIN.

THAT'S WHY THE LOCALS NEED *US* ON CASES LIKE THIS.

WE'RE TRAINED OBSERVERS.

HEY! *OBSERVERS!* THAT'S THE *SKIN* GUY!

CONTACT THE NEAREST ARMY BASE. TELL THEM WE'RE ON THE *HULK'S* TRAIL...

AND THAT WE'LL NEED *ALL* AVAILABLE TROOPS.

BINGO.

WAM
WAM
WAM

NOW *STOP* THAT BANGING THIS INST-- *ELIZABETH!*

SISTER, WE *HAVE* TO SEE THE REVEREND MOTHER, RIGHT AWAY!

YES, YES, OF COURSE.

I KNOW IT'S ASKING A *LOT*, REVEREND MOTHER-- BUT PLEASE, *PLEASE* HIDE US. JUST FOR A *SHORT* TIME. JUST TO GIVE THINGS TIME TO CALM DOWN.

MM HMM, SOOO...

YOU'RE BETTY'S LATE HUSBAND.

YES, MA'AM.

YOU'RE NOT EXACTLY WHAT I EXPECTED.

I'M NEVER WHAT *ANYONE* EXPECTS.

DON'T TAKE THIS WRONG, YOUNG MAN, BUT... WHY AREN'T YOU *DEAD?*

I DON'T *KNOW*, FRANKLY. WHATEVER HAPPENED THAT SAVED ME FROM THE GAMMA BOMB EX-PLOSION SOMEHOW PUT ME OUT OF COMMISSION FOR SEVERAL MONTHS, AND PLACED THE HULK IN *TOTAL* CHARGE.

BUT WHAT WAS THE HULK *DOING* DURING THOSE MONTHS, BRUCE?

HE... UH...

...HE...

I DON'T KNOW.

SORRY. SOUND LIKE A BROKEN RECORD.

IT DOESN'T MATTER. WHAT MATTERS IS THAT WE'VE *FOUND* EACH OTHER, AND *NOTHING* IS GOING TO SEPARATE US AGAIN.

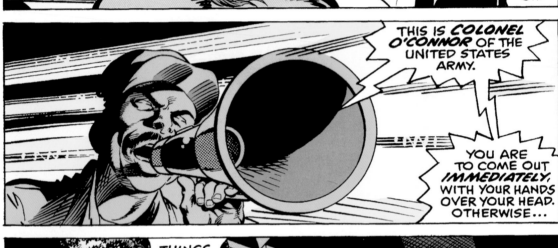

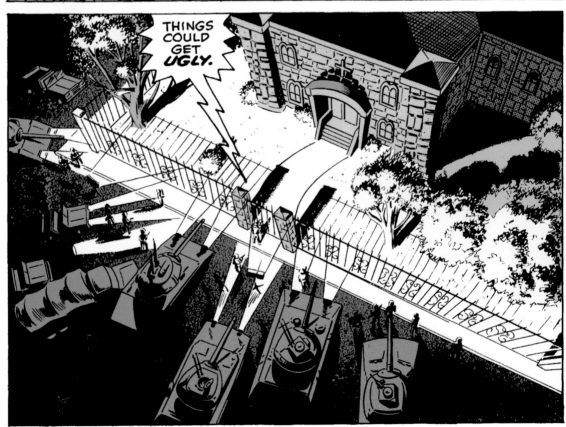

THAT'S NOT THE *POINT*, MA'AM.

RESPECT IS RESPECT, AND THAT MOST CERTAINLY *IS* THE POINT, AND I'M *CERTAIN* THAT'S WHAT YOU WERE TAUGHT. AND IF YOU HAD SPOKEN TO YOUR *TEACHERS* IN THIS FASHION, YOU WOULD HAVE GOTTEN YOUR *KNUCKLES* RAPPED.

AND I HAVE A *RULER* ON MY DESK!

PROBLEM, COLONEL?

YOU'D, UH, HAVE TO HAVE GONE TO CATHOLIC SCHOOL TO *UNDERSTAND*, DOCTOR.

INTIMIDATED BY *NUNS*, EH? COMMON PHOBIA FOR CATHOLIC SCHOOL GRADS.

NOW *ME*...I ATTENDED A *YESHIVA*. I'M FINE UNLESS A VERY STRICT *RABBI* SHOWS UP.

MA'AM, WITH *ALL* DUE RESPECT, WE'LL WAIT FOREVER IF WE HAVE TO, BUT THE BANNERS ARE *NOT* LEAVING.

LEONARD SAMSON'S HERE, TOO! OH, BRUCE, WHAT ARE WE--

UNNHHHHH...

BRUCE?

BRU--

OH.

I CAN'T BELIEVE ...THAT I FORGOT.

MA'AM, YOU CAN'T BELIEVE THE POWER OF THE INDIVIDUAL YOU'RE DEALING WITH. YOU MUST HAVE SOME QUESTIONS.

YES I DO.

WHY IS YOUR HAIR GREEN?

STEROIDS.

UH OH. I JUST REALIZED.

AGENT COOPER! THE SUN'S GONE DOWN.

DON'T WORRY ABOUT IT, DOCTOR SAMSON.

OUR INTELLIGENCE REPORTS THAT BANNER HAS REVERTED TO THE GREEN HULK SCENARIO, WITH ANGER TRIGGERING THE CHANGE.

THAT'S WHY WE'RE PROCEEDING CAREFULLY... WITH THIS TRANQ RIFLE HERE FOR BACKUP. THE GRAY HULK, DAY/NIGHT SCENARIO IS OBVIOUSLY PASSE. AFTER ALL...

THE GREEN AND GRAY HULKS CAN'T CO-EXIST.

OH, OF COURSE.

THEY COULDN'T POSSIBLY CO-EXIST.

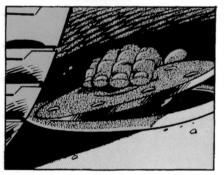

WAIT A MINUTE.

BANNER'S A MULTIPLE PERSONALITY.

WHY CAN'T THEY CO-EXIST?

HEY!

SIGMUND FREUD!

WHAT'RE YOU *STARING* AT?

I'VE STARTED USING GRECIAN FORMULA TO GET THE GRAY OUT, OKAY? NOW LET'S GO.

I DON'T KNOW, I...

YOU LOOK *DIFFERENT* SOMEHOW.

ELIZABETH! MY CHILD, MY...

MY OFFICE.

MY LORD.

REVEREND MOTHER, I'M SO *SORRY* ABOUT ALL THIS. I HATE TO *LEAVE* YOU THIS WAY BUT...

IT'S ALL RIGHT. JUST *GO.*

I CAUGHT THIS GOBLET.

THANK YOU. IT HAS SENTIMENTAL VALUE. NOW GO.

AND YOUR *DESK* IS STILL STANDING, YOU CAN HARDLY *SEE* THE BULLET HOLES...

JUST *GO.* NOW.

THANK YOU AGAIN...

GO. GOOD-BYE.

KRASH

THIS WAS A *TEST,* WASN'T IT?

HULK... WAIT...

I JUST WANTED TO *HELP...*

SOMEHOW, DOCTOR, I GET THE FEELING HE DOESN'T *WANT* YOUR HELP.

I THOUGHT YOU WERE DEAD.

YEAH, WELL WE MONSTERS ALWAYS COME BACK IN *SEQUELS*. AND THAT'S ALL I *AM* TO YOU, RIGHT?

A MONSTER. AN UGLY SIDE OF YOUR HUSBAND.

I'M LIKE *ALCOHOLISM*. YOU LOVE BANNER, BUT HE'S GOT THIS HUGE PROBLEM THAT YOU'RE *STUCK* WITH. IT MAKES YOU *HATE* ME, DOESN'T IT?

WHAT DID YOU DO FOR ALL THOSE MONTHS, HULK?

NONE OF YOUR *BUSINESS*. ANSWER THE QUESTION.

I *DON'T* HATE YOU. I'VE SPENT THE PAST FEW MONTHS LEARNING HOW *NOT* TO HATE. LEARNING THAT THERE MUST BE REASONS FOR EVERYTHING-- EVEN *MONSTERS*.

YEAH, WELL, MAYBE *I* HATE *YOU*.

NO. YOU'RE *AFRAID* OF ME.

HAH!

IT'S *TRUE.* YOU'RE AFRAID BECAUSE YOU FEEL *AFFECTION* FOR ME, AND THAT MAKES YOU JUST LIKE "PUNY BANNER."

SO WE'RE BOTH TANGLED IN CLUMSY EMOTIONS. BUT... BUT MAYBE LIKE ALCOHOLICS AND THEIR FAMILIES, WE CAN FORM OUR OWN *SUPPORT* GROUP TO *DEAL* WITH THINGS.

IF WE CAN'T *LOVE* EACH OTHER, AT LEAST WE CAN TRY TO *TOLER-ATE* EACH OTHER. MAY-BE... EVEN *HELP* EACH OTHER?

WHO DO YOU THINK YOU'RE *TALK*ING TO? A BOY SCOUT? CRIPES!

SUPPORT GROUPS! YOU'RE *NUTS!* I CAN JUST *SEE* IT. "HELLO, MY NAME IS THE HULK. I'M A GAMMA-IRRADI-ATED MONSTER, I ADMIT IT FREELY."

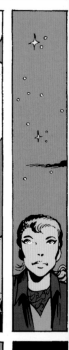

HEH. HEH HEH...

HEE HEEE HEEE

WHAT'S SO BLASTED *FUNNY?*

I'M,...I'M JUST PICTURING... YOU AND ABOMINATION...

....AND... AND THE *LEADER*... ON LITTLE FOLDING CHAIRS IN A CIRCLE...

HAH HAH HAH!

YOU'VE REALLY *LOST* IT. YOU...

HEH. LITTLE CHAIRS... THAT...

...THAT KEEP *BREAKING* UNDER US...

HAAH HA

HA HEH

HA HA

OOOHHH ...OH THAT FELT GOOD.

YEAH.

SURRENDER, JONES! YOU'RE ONLY EXACERBATING THE SITUATION!

YEAH? WELL, I DON'T KNOW THE *MEANING* OF THE WORD!

IT MEANS "GIVE UP."

WELL, SURE, I KNEW *THAT.*

WHUMP

IT'S *"EXACERBATING"* THAT'S GOT ME STUMPED.

IT MEANS YOU'RE ONLY MAKING IT *HARDER* ON YOURSELF.

THANKS FOR CLEARING THAT UP.

KRUNCH

NUTS. THAT WAS MY FAVORITE *GUITAR.*

YOU LOOK A LITTLE OUT OF BREATH.

OUT OF *BREATH!* I THOUGHT I WAS OUT OF MY *MIND*, LIKE THE *REST* OF THE PEOPLE IN THIS 'BURB!

FOLLOW: I COME TO THIS TOWN TO DO AN AUTOGRAPH SESSION FOR MY BOOK, *SIDEKICK*... YOU *READ* IT?

NOT YET.

IT'S *BRUTAL. ANY* WHO, THIS WHOLE TOWN'S TURNED INTO "INVASION OF THE BODY SNATCHERS." THEY'VE ALL WEIRDED *OUT* ON ME.

Y'KNOW, I'D HEARD YOU WERE *HUMAN.* OBVIOUSLY YOU CHANGED *BACK.* LOOKS *GOOD* ON YOU.

SO, WHAT'S OUR FIRST MOVE?

WAP

"SIDEKICK: MY LIFE IN THE SUPER HERO BIZ," BY RICK JONES, SO THE WORM'S A *BOOKWORM* NOW. LESSEE...

"SOMETIMES I'D LIE AWAKE IN THE ORPHANAGE AND TRY TO PICTURE WHAT MY PARENTS LOOKED LIKE. AS I'VE GONE THROUGH LIFE, I'D TRADE ALL THE WONDERS I'VE SEEN JUST TO GLIMPSE THEIR FACES."

SO HE DOESN'T REMEMBER HIS FOLKS. HE'S *LUCKY.* THEY MIGHTA BEEN LIKE...

LIKE *WHAT?*

NOTHIN'. SKIP IT. I DON'T READ BOOKS, ANYWAY. I'LL WAIT FOR THE MOVIE.

THEY BETTER GET *ARNOLD* TO PLAY ME OR THERE'LL BE TROUBLE.

AND WHAT'RE *YOU* UP TO?

CHECKING MAPS. BRUCE AND I TALKED DURING THE DAY, AND DECIDED WE SHOULD FIND RICK.

HE KNOWS *LOTS* OF PEOPLE. HE'LL KNOW THE BEST WAY TO PROCEED...

FORGET IT! I DON'T NEED *ANYBODY.*

OH, REALLY? OKAY, FINE! *LEAVE.* I CAN'T STOP YOU. JUST *GO.*

SPLOOOSH

COUGH
SPUTTER

RUN! *ATLANTIS* IS *ATTACKING* AGAIN!

OH. *I* SEE. SOMEONE GAVE ME A 10-GALLON WAKE UP CALL.

ALL RIGHT! I THINK I SHOULD *WARN* YOU-- I *KNOW* PEOPLE! PEOPLE WITH *SERIOUS* BICEPS AND *FUNKY* COSTUMES! AND THEY'LL GET ME *OUT* OF HERE, AND BEAT THE SNOT OUT OF *YOU* WHILE THEY'RE AT IT!

BUT IF YOU KICK ME LOOSE NOW, WE'LL JUST *FORGET* THIS HAPPENED. WE GOT A DEAL?

UNNHH. GUESS NOT.

COME *ON*, MAN, DOUSE THE SPOTLIGHT. I MAY WANT TO USE MY RETINAS AGAIN SOMEDAY.

WHAT'S THIS JOINT *ABOUT*, ANYWAY? WHO *ARE* YOU?

CHILL, MAN. IT'S ONLY ME.

THE PAIN IN THE NECK. THE MONKEY IN THE WRENCH.

YOUR OLD PAL, *RICK JONES.*

YEAH... YEAH, RIGHT.... AND I'M FREDRIC WERTHAM.

IF YOU THINK I'M *BUYING* THIS...

THEN BUY *THIS!* I'M THE BIG, BRAVE BOZO WHO DESTROYED BRUCE BANNER'S LIFE! HOW'S *THAT* GRAB YOU, "FRED"?

WAP

I *DIDN'T* DESTROY HIS LIFE, YOU XEROXED ZOMBIE. SURE, SURE...

I WAS IN THE *WRONG* PLACE AT THE *WRONG* TIME. BUT IT WAS AN *ACCIDENT.* IT WAS--

ACCIDENT! YOU FEEB! I WAS *THERE,* REMEMBER? I HAD TO BE THE BIG SHOT WHO BET THE OTHER GUYS I COULD SNEAK ONTO THE TESTING GROUNDS!

WAK

I WAS THE ONE WHO FORCED BRUCE BANNER TO SAVE ME AND TURNED HIM INTO A GAMMA SPONGE! *I* DID!

NO YOU DIDN'T! IT WAS *ME! YOU'RE* NOT ME! *I* AM!

SO *YOU'RE* THE IDIOT WHO DID ALL THAT, THEN?

YES! IT WAS...

IT WAS *ME,* OKAY?

I *RUINED* BRUCE'S LIFE.

HAPPY?

ONE HUNDRED EIGHTY THOUSAND TWENTY SEVEN SHEEP...

ONE HUNDRED EIGHTY THOUSAND TWENTY EIGHT SHEEP...

ONE HUNDRED EIGHTY THOUSAND TWENTY N--

thup a thup

≒YAWWWN≒

BRUCE? DID YOU GET ANY SLEEP?

I'M *FINE.* LET'S GO. WE'VE LAIN AROUND LONG ENOUGH.

LONG ENOUGH? BRUCE, HEAVENS, IT'S ONLY 9 AM! AND WE ONLY LAY DOWN AT SUNRISE, AFTER THE HULK TRAVELED ALL NIGHT. AND--

WHAT THE HULK DID OR DID *NOT* DO IS OF *NO* INTEREST TO ME! DO YOU UNDERSTAND? AND WE'RE NOT GOING TO ACCOMPLISH *ANYTHING* BY WASTING TIME *SLEEPING!* IS THAT *CLEAR*, BETTY?

DID HE SLEEP AT *ALL?*

"HEY RICK, WAKE UP."

OH, WHAT *NOW?* THE GHOST OF CHRISTMAS PRESENT? GIMME A BREAK...

YOU WANT A *BREAK?* I SHOULD GIVE THE BETRAYER A BREAK...

MY OLD BUCKY COSTUME?

WHAT'S THIS *"BETRAYER"* JAZZ? I NEVER--

AND *ROM!*

AND *BETTY!*

ARRGHH!

THAT'S FOR WHEN I DITCHED CAP!

ARRHH!

AND *THAT'S* FOR DITCHING MAR-VELL!

UNNHHH!

WE'VE BEEN A *USER,* ALL OUR LIVES. THAT'S ALL. A USER.

I HANG OUT WITH PEOPLE, USE 'EM TILL I'M *DONE* AND THEN GO OFF TO THE *NEXT* ADVENTURE, LEAVING A TRAIL OF BROKEN BODIES AND RESPONSIBILITIES BEHIND ME.

Not you... ME...

cracked ...rib... I think...

please... stop... stop...

I THINK HE'S UN-CONSCIOUS.

WOULDN'T SURPRISE ME.

DID YOU *HAVE* TO MENTION MAR-VELL? JUST HEARING HIS NAME FILLS ME WITH *DISGUST.*

BE DISGUSTED. JUST REMEMBER WHAT OUR *GOAL* IS.

OH, I REMEMBER WELL ENOUGH.

BUT I DO *NOT* HAVE TO LIKE IT.

THIS IS ALL *VERY* PECULIAR. THAT NEWSPAPERMAN WE CALLED IN THE NEXT TOWN OVER-- HE SAID BUNKPORT WAS PRACTICALLY A *GHOST TOWN* SINCE THE BOTTOM FELL OUT OF THE LOCAL INDUSTRY...

AND FROM THE LACK OF LOCAL POPULATION, I'D SAY HE WAS *RIGHT*.

BUT THEN WHY WOULD THEY INSIST ON RICK SHOWING UP FOR A SIGNING? WHY--?

AH. I THINK I SEE THE PLACE FOR ANSWERS, THERE'S A *BOOKSTORE*.

VAS NO NTION

BOOKS

VISA

VAS NO NTION

BOOKS

Jing Jing

HELLO? IS ANYBODY--?

BELLS, HOW QUAINT.

VISA

FICTION

RICK JONES

KICK.

NOT GONNA *BE* A SIGNING, PUNK NEVER *SHOWED*.

IRRESPONSIBLE KID, GUESS HE HAD *BETTER* THINGS TO DO THAN KEEP HIS WORD.

AH! HELLO! WE'RE HERE FOR THE SIGNING...?

KNOW WHAT? I THINK YOU'RE *LYING*, BECAUSE RICK JONES WOULDN'T SIMPLY "NOT SHOW UP," YOU PUG-UGLY *TROGLODYTE*.

NONE OF THIS SMELLS RIGHT...

AND IF YOU PEOPLE ARE *UP* TO SOMETHING, THEN HEAVEN *HELP* YOU.

BRUCE!

BRUCE, WHAT WAS *THAT* ALL ABOUT? WHY ARE YOU *BEING* LIKE THIS?

BECAUSE I'VE DECIDED THAT I'M TIRED OF THE WORLD DOING WHATEVER IT WANTS TO ME AND MINE. I WOULD *THINK*, BETTY, THAT *YOU* OF ALL PEOPLE WOULD *APPRECIATE* THAT.

I APPRECIATE THAT IF YOU DON'T GET A GOOD FEW HOURS SLEEP, YOU'RE GOING TO GO *CRAZY!*

BETTY... SWEETHEART... MY *DEAREST* LOVE...

YOU'RE TALKING TO A MAN WHO PRESENTLY HAS *THREE* PERSONALITIES.

WHAT MAKES YOU THINK I'M NOT CRAZY *NOW?*

WHO ARE YOU?

I'm... RICK JONES... I'm the PARTNER OF...

I'm RICK JONES, I...

SO MANY YOU'VE HURT AND USED.

OF WHOM?

IN YOUR SEARCH FOR YOUR IDENTITY, YOU'VE DESERTED AND BETRAYED SO MANY PEOPLE, WHO DO YOU THINK YOU ARE, TO DO THAT?

SO MANY IDENTITIES. NO WONDER YOU HUNG OUT WITH MASKED MEN, WHO HIDE THEMSELVES.

YOU DON'T KNOW YOUR OWN IDENTITY.

BETRAYER IN HERO'S CLOTHES, LIFE-DESTROYER, ALWAYS PRETENDING TO SOMETHING ELSE. WHO ARE YOU? WHAT ARE YOU?

I...DON'T KNOW...

I DON'T KNOW... ANYMORE...

BRUCE... THE FEW PEOPLE WE SEE... THEY'RE STARING AT US, LIKE WE'RE FROM ANOTHER *PLANET.*

IGNORE THEM.

BRUCE? ARE YOU *SURE* WE SHOULD GO IN HERE?

BRUCE?

EXCUSE ME! I SAID *EXCUSE* ME!

RICK JONES WAS SUPPOSED TO COME TO THIS ARMPIT OF A TOWN TO SIGN AUTOGRAPHS. HE'S *VANISHED.* WHY AREN'T YOU *LOOKING* FOR HIM?

RICK! RICK JONES!

NEVER *HEARD* OF ANY NICK JONES.

LOOK, TAKE *OFF,* YOU SLOB. I TOLD YOU, I DON'T *KNOW* NICK.

WHAT ARE YOU, STUPID *AND* DEAF?

PUSH *OFF,* MISTER. I'M *WARNING* YOU.

PUSH OFF! I'LL PUSH THIS WHOLE *TOWN* DOWN AROUND YOUR *EARS!*

WE'RE *LEAVING,* BRUCE! *NOW!*

BRUCE, THIS ISN'T HELPING *ANYTHING!* YOU'RE GOING TO GET US *ARRESTED!* AND WOULDN'T THE GOVERNMENT JUST *LOVE* TO KNOW WHERE YOU ARE! SO THEY CAN MAKE SURE THE HULK WILL NEVER MENACE ANYONE AGAIN!

THEY'RE *HIDING* SOMETHING! THEY'RE *LYING* TO ME! I *WON'T* BE LIED TO, AND--

MISTER?

HEY, MISTER? YOU LOOKING FOR YOUR *FRIEND?* THE NICE MAN WITH THE BROWN HAIR?

UH...YES, YES, I AM.

I CAN *TAKE* YOU TO HIM. HE'S IN A BAD PLACE.

"BAD PLACE?" *WHERE*, HONEY? WHAT'S *HAPPENING* IN THIS TOWN?

I DON'T KNOW, *HONEST*, I DON'T KNOW. BUT EVERY-BODY IS BEING REALLY *DIFFERENT.*

AND I WANT THEM TO *STOP.* IF I TAKE YOU TO THE BAD PLACE WHERE YOUR FRIEND IS, WILL YOU MAKE THEM *STOP?*

ABSOLUTELY.

I THINK HE'S *READY.* HIS MIND SHOULD BE PLIABLE ENOUGH NOW THAT WE CAN GET FROM IT WHAT WE WANT.

MAKE SURE EVERYTHING IS *PREPARED.* I'LL BRING HIM ALONG IN A FEW MOMENTS.

WHO WOULD HAVE THOUGHT SOMEONE LIKE YOU WOULD BE *WORTH* ALL THIS TIME AND TROUBLE? OR THAT SOMEONE WITH A MIND LIKE YOURS COULD BE BROKEN SO *EASILY?*

WAAM

APPARENTLY SOMEONE AS DUMB AS *YOU* THOUGHT IT!

UNNNHHH!

YOU THINK AFTER THE LIFE *I'VE* LED, YOUR LITTLE "CLOCK-WORK ORANGE" RIFF WORKED? THAT WAS *NOTHING.* TRY COUNT-ING TO FIVE BILLION WHILE HANGING IN THE *NEGATIVE ZONE. THERE'S* A CHALLENGE IN KEEPING YOUR HEAD SCREWED ON.

OH, AND WHEN YOU'RE CAP'S PARTNER, YOU LEARN TO TAKE *PUNCHES* ...AND SLIP ROPES.

HOOOLEEEE COW. I DON'T *BELIEVE* WHAT I'M SEEING.

THIS IS A SKRULL OUTPOST. I'VE BEEN CAPTURED BY ALIENS.

GREAT. LIKE I NEEDED THIS.

YOU! SOLDIER! WHY ARE YOU STILL WEARING THE UGLY HUMAN FORM OF RICK JONES?

UHHH... IT'S STUCK.

STUCK?! WHAT IN THE NEBULA ARE YOU TALKING AB--

COMMANDER! LOOK!

IT APPEARS THE SUPER SKRULL IS ABOUT TO DISPATCH SOME INTRUDERS!

THEY WERE ASKING ALL OVER TOWN ABOUT JONES, PERHAPS...

YESSS...I KNOW WHAT YOU'RE GOING TO SAY. WE SHOULD BRING THE *REAL* JONES OUT HERE TO VIEW THEIR DEATH.

NOTHING WILL PRODUCE QUITE AS MUCH STRESS IN HIM AS WATCHING FELLOW HUMANS DIE. AND *HOPEFULLY*...

THAT STRESS WILL STIMULATE HIS MIND TO DISPLAY THE MIND POWER HE ONCE WIELDED, SO THAT WE CAN *TAP* IT. THAT *IS* OUR MISSION, AFTER ALL.

"DISPLAY HIS POWER?" YOU MEAN THE MIND POWER THAT ENDED THE KREE-SKRULL WAR? BUT...

BUT THAT WAS THE INTELLIGENCE SUPREME *PUSHING* HIM INTO THAT! HE COULD *NEVER* DO IT ON HIS OWN.

THAT, SOLDIER, IS FOR OUR *MISSION* TO DECIDE. AND I'M SURPRISED YOU WOULD QUESTION ORDERS.

WHAT?

INTRIGUING. INFERIOR BEINGS HAVE *SCREAMED* WHEN THEY FACED ME. FOUGHT ME, CURSED ME, FAINTED DEAD AWAY.

NONE HAS EVER EXPRESSED CONCERN FOR MY WELFARE.

HOW *AMUSING.*

STAY *AWAY* FROM HIM! PLEASE! FOR YOUR OWN SAFETY!

*IN ISSUE #368. --BOBBIE.

"MY MOST RECENT INVOLVED A COWARDLY ASSAULT BY AN ATTACKER WHO THOUGHT HE HAD MORTALLY WOUNDED ME. HE LEFT ME FOR DEAD."

"ACTUALLY, I WAS IN A DEEP, HEALING COMA, AS IS CUSTOMARY FOR MY KIND WHEN FRIGHTFULLY INJURED."

"THE CURSED SILVER SURFER ALSO THOUGHT ME DEAD AND THOUGHT THAT, BY DROPPING ME INTO A PLANET'S ATMOSPHERE, I WOULD BE CREMATED AS BEFITS A WARRIOR."

"WHAT HE DIDN'T *REALIZE* WAS THAT THE FRICTION OF RE-ENTRY MERELY ACTIVATED THE POWERS OF THE HUMAN TORCH, FOR I CARRY WITHIN ME THE POWERS OF ALL THE FANTASTIC FOUR."

"I BEGAN TO IGNITE, HASTENING MY RECOVERY. BECAUSE I WAS FULLY AFLAME, HOWEVER..."

"I WAS PICKED UP BY A SHIP THAT HAD BEEN FOLLOWING MY MISHAPS AND WITNESSING MY 'DEATH'. THEY GLEEFULLY ANTICIPATED DISSECTING ME TO LEARN MY SECRETS."

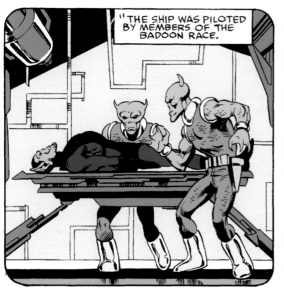

"THE SHIP WAS PILOTED BY MEMBERS OF THE BADOON RACE."

"I STRESS THE WORD *WAS!*"

ELSEWHERE...

I'M NOT QUESTIONING ORDERS. ALL I'M SAYING IS...UH...

...THAT YOU'RE NOT GOING TO ACTIVATE THOSE POWERS WITHOUT REALLY SHOCKING HIM. JUST SHOWING DEATH ON A SCREEN IS NOTHING. THEY HAVE THAT ON EARTH ALL THE TIME. IT'S CALLED "TELEVISION."

YOU KNOW, I THINK YOU'RE RIGHT, FIRST OFFICER-- ORDER THE SUPER SKRULL TO *RETURN* WITH HIS CAPTIVES.

SO YOU SEE, WOMAN, IF I CAN SURVIVE ALL *THAT*...I THINK I CAN HANDLE YOU.

IT'S NOTHING PERSONAL. WE WANT TO DEFEAT THE KREE. IT'S JUST THAT YOU HUMANS ALWAYS SEEM TO GET IN THE WAY.

THIS >ACK< IS A BIG MISTAKE!

SO YOU KEEP SAYING.

SUPER SKRULL! OUR COMMANDER ORDERS YOU TO RETURN TO THE SHIP, WITH THE CAPTIVES ALIVE!

WHAT? *NONSENSE.* THEY'RE MY CAPTIVES, AND I SHALL DIS- POSE OF THEM AS I WISH.

THE COMMANDER WAS MOST EXPLICIT.

I TIRE OF YOUR COMMANDER'S ARROGANCE. HE DOESN'T KNOW WHO HE'S DEALING WITH.

BUT I THINK I WILL *SHOW* HIM. *NOW.*

FIRST THE *WOMAN*, BECAUSE OF HER *LUDICROUS* CLAIMS OF *CONCERN* FOR ME. THEN THE *MAN*.

PATHETIC EARTHLINGS...

WHO WILL SAVE YOU NOW?

HULK...PLEASE... BETTY IS...

CHOOSE, BANNER. HER OR ME.

ALL...

ALL RIGHT...

AWRIGHT.

AWRIGHT!!

RIIIIPPP

PARDON ME FOR *NOT* BEING *IMPRESSED* BY AN ERSATZ THING. I'VE GONE TOE-TO-TOE WITH THE *GENUINE* ARTICLE, AND BELIEVE ME...

THERE AIN'T *NOTHING* LIKE THE *REAL THING,* BABY.

YOU *MOCK* ME!!

JOE'S

147

YOU'RE *QUICK,* Y'KNOW THAT?

GRAY-SKINNED BUFFOON! I AM THE *GREATEST* WARRIOR IN THE SKRULL ARMY!

THEN THEY MUST *NOT* HAVE A REAL *PICKY* ENLISTMENT OFFICE.

KRASH

YOU SEEM TO BE UNDER THE IMPRESSION THAT YOU'RE SOMETHING *SPECIAL,* HULK.

OOOOF!

YOU'RE FACING AN OPPONENT WHOSE HOME IS IN THE *STARS!*

HOPE THE HULK'S DOING OKAY.

WHAT AM I SAYING? I HOPE *I'M* DOING OKAY.

RICK!

HUH?

IT'S ALL RIGHT, SON. THE *AVENGERS* ARE HERE NOW.

IT'S JUST A MATTER OF MOPPING UP.

CAP! BOY OH BOY...

YOU CAN'T BELIEVE HOW *HAPPY* I AM TO SEE YOU...

BECAUSE IT JUST CONFIRMS FOR ME THAT SKRULLS AREN'T GETTING ANY *SMARTER.*

EMPRESS!

OR DID YOU *REAL-LY* THINK YOU'D CATCH ME TWICE WITH THE SAME STUNT?

ALL *RIGHT* THEN, JONES...

YOU SHALL SEE...

THE SUNLIGHT'S STILL SLOWING ME DOWN. I'VE MADE *HEADWAY* IN BEING THE DOMINANT PERSONA, BUT BANNER'S MAKING IT *TOUGH*.

FORTUNATELY, THAT STAR WARS REJECT DOESN'T *KNOW* WHAT I'M GOING THR--

OOOOOOFFFF!!

KLA-THOOM

HEY!

COME *OUT!* FIGHT LIKE A *WHATEVER!*

FOOL. THIS IS ONE OF MY *GREATEST* WEAPONS: *INVISIBILITY!*

YEAH, AND I BET YOU USE IT TO SNEAK INTO GIRLS' LOCKER ROOMS.

THAT'S WHAT *I'D* DO.

WHAT YOU WILL DO... IS *DIE!*

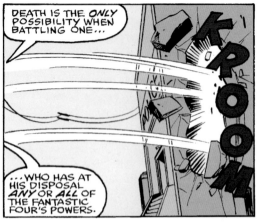

DEATH IS THE *ONLY* POSSIBILITY WHEN BATTLING ONE...

KROOM

...WHO HAS AT HIS DISPOSAL *ANY* OR *ALL* OF THE FANTASTIC FOUR'S POWERS.

HE KEEPS BOASTING ABOUT THAT, BUT WHAT *I* DON'T GET...

...IS WHY HE JUST *DOESN'T* USE *ALL* OF THEM, *ALL* THE *TIME*.

YOU'VE STOPPED MOVING. DOES THAT MEAN YOU'VE SEEN THE *INEVITABILITY* OF YOUR DEFEAT?

IT MUST TAX HIS STRENGTH. HE MUST BE *LIMITED* THAT WAY. USING EACH POWER *DRAINS* HIM...

SO HE PICKS AND CHOOSES. AND THAT MEANS HE *WON'T* USE A POWER...

...UNLESS HE KNOWS HE'LL *NEED* IT. SO IF I CAN SNAP THIS BAR FROM THE CELL DOOR WITHOUT HIM *SPOTTING* IT...

NO MORE *BOASTS*, EH?

THE STRENGTH OF THE THING, WHICH YOU MOCKED EARLIER, WILL BE ENOUGH TO FINISH YOU, SURELY.

ARRRRGGHHHH!

SLUGH

WRONG. AND DON'T CALL ME "SHIRLEY."

UNHH!

PARDON ME, COMING THROUGH.

THERE HE IS!

DON'T *SHOOT* HIM! STRAY SHOTS COULD...

QUIET!

COULD *WHAT?* HIT THESE *CONTROLS?*

AND *THEN* WHAT HAPPENS?

UH OH.

R U M

MBLLLL

HULK! WHY IS THE *GROUND* SHAKING?!

BECAUSE MY LIFE ISN'T *EXCITING* ENOUGH, *THAT'S* WHY.

GET *AWAY* FROM THERE!

DRY UP, FROG FACE. HECK, THIS ISN'T MUCH MORE COMPLICATED THAN MY OLD *CHEVY.*

OKAY. IF YOU *INSIST.*

BKOW

THINK I STUNNED HIM. NOW TO GET OUTTA--

BETTY!!

HULK! BRUCE! HELP *MEEEEE!*

ME OR BRUCE, WHO DO YOU WANT HOLDING YOU WHEN YOU LAND FROM 1000 FEET UP?

YOU.

GOOD CALL.

SOMETHING'S FALLEN INTO THE ENERGY CORE, COMMANDER! IT'S *RUPTURED!* OVERLOAD COMMENCING!

WE ONLY HAVE *SECONDS* LEFT, COMMANDER! WHAT DO WE *DO?!*

WE EXPLODE.

RAKOVLAAM

HULK...RICK MUST HAVE BEEN CAPTURED BY THEM...HE WAS *ON* THAT SHIP...

YEAH, WELL... IT'S...

IT'S NOT LIKE I *CARE* ABOUT... ABOUT...

RICK... MY *FRIEND*...

OHHH, BETTY ...HE'S *GONE!* AFTER ALL WE'VE BEEN THROUGH, RICK'S...

HI, GUYS, MISS ME?

DON'T LOOK SO SHOCKED. I ALWAYS CARRY A MINIATURE *PARACHUTE* WITH ME, IN CASE I HAVE TO JUMP FROM AN EXPLODING SKRULL SAUCER.

THAT'S...THAT'S *RIDICULOUS*,

WHY? I *NEEDED* TO, DIDN'T I?

YES, BUT...

SKIP IT.

YOU'RE LOOKING PRETTY HEALTHY FOR A DEAD MAN, BRUCE. BY THE WAY, IT'S *NIGHT.* WHERE'S THE *HULK?*

I DON'T KNOW. I DON'T KNOW WHAT *ANY* OF IT MEANS, EXCEPT THAT MAYBE FOR THE FIRST TIME IN AGES, I CAN GET SOME SLEEP.

GOOD DEAL. COME ON, LET'S GET TO THE HIGHWAY AND HITCH A RIDE. I'VE *HAD* IT WITH THIS BOOK TOUR JAZZ. I WANNA GO *HOME.*

I'VE GOT A NEW APARTMENT IN RENO. THERE'S A SWIMMING POOL...

"...AND I GOT A HOT NEW GIRL-FRIEND I BET YOU GUYS'LL *LOVE.*"

KNOK

IF YOU'RE LOOKING FOR GOD'S GIFT TO WOMEN, HE'S STILL ON HIS BOOK TOUR.

MR. FLIRTATION, THAT'S *RICK,* ALL RIGHT.

I'LL TELL HIM YOU CAME BY MISS...?

CHANDLER. *MARLO* CHANDLER.

I'M HIS GIRL-FRIEND.

4A

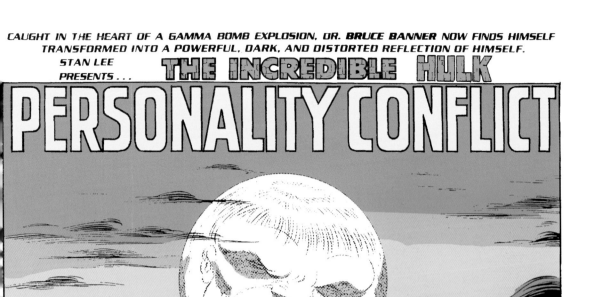

I SAID *QUIET*, BLAST IT. I MEAN *NOW*.

YOU'VE GOT TO *STOP* THIS! I'M *WARNING* YOU...

OH, I'M *SOOOO* SCARED, YOU *NEED* US, BUDDY BOY. *REMEMBER* THAT.

NEED NO ONE. ALL *PUNY.* ALL *FOOLS.*

STOP IT! STOP IT THIS *SEC*--

NYUNNNHHH...

OH MY DEAR *LORD!*

⸝ YAWN ⸜

BRUCE?

YOU *AWAKE*, MAN?

ALL RIGHT, PROMETHEUS. TELL US IN YOUR *OWN* WORDS JUST WHAT HAPPENED.

MY OWN WORDS.

HOW ABOUT, "I GOT MY *BUTT* KICKED."

THIS WAS A SIMPLE *SEARCH* AND *SEIZE* OPERATION, PROMETHEUS. HOW COULD YOU *BLOW* IT SO BADLY?

JOB ALWAYS LOOKS EASIER FROM THE *OTHER* SIDE OF THE TABLE, PARIS. FROM WHERE *I* WAS SITTING... WHICH WAS BEHIND THE WHEEL OF A CAR EQUIPPED TO HANDLE THE *GRAY* HULK...

I WAS LUCKY TO GET AWAY *ALIVE*.

SO WHAT HAPPENED, PRO?

WHAT HAPPENED, ATALANTA, WAS THAT I WOUND UP TUSSLING WITH THE *GREEN* HULK INSTEAD. MY GIMMICKS COULDN'T TAKE HIM, OR EVEN *SLOW* HIM.

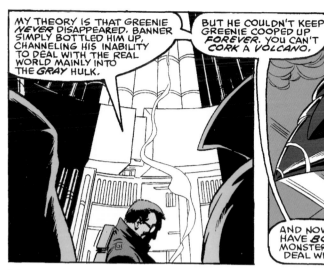

MY THEORY IS THAT GREENIE *NEVER* DISAPPEARED. BANNER SIMPLY BOTTLED HIM UP, CHANNELING HIS INABILITY TO DEAL WITH THE REAL WORLD MAINLY INTO THE *GRAY* HULK.

BUT HE COULDN'T KEEP GREENIE COOPED UP *FOREVER*. YOU CAN'T *CORK* A *VOLCANO*.

AND NOW WE HAVE *BOTH* MONSTERS TO DEAL WITH.

RECOMMENDATIONS?

WELL WELL WELL

LOOK WHO *DEE*-CIDED TO PUT IN AN APPEARANCE.

YOU WANT *MY* RECOMMENDATION, AGAMEMNON? FINE.

WE *TAKE* HIM. HIS STRENGTH WOULD BE INVALUABLE, AND IF WE CAN DO SOMETHING WITH HIS MIND...

THEN HE... AND *WE*... WOULD BE *UNSTOPPABLE*.

THAT, AGGY, IS MY RECOMMENDATION.

NO IFS, ANDS...

...OR *BUTTS*.

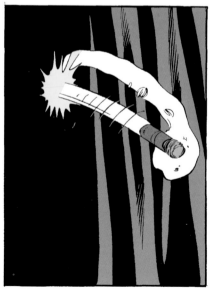

AAARRH!

RICK! THAT WAS--

KISS THE COOK

I KNOW. IT'S BRUCE.

HE SAID HE WAS GONNA TRY AND SLEEP. COME *ON*.

MAN, I HOPE HE'S NOT *CHANGING*.

I JUST HAD THE PLACE *PAINTED*.

THEY'RE... THEY'RE *GONE*.

WHO? *WHO'S GONE*? SOMEONE WAS *IN* HERE?

THE HULKS... THE GRAY HULK WENT TO CONFRONT THE GREEN...

AND MY MIND... SEALED THEM *OFF*, AS IF TO *PROTECT* ME.

...MAYBE MAYBE THEY'RE GOING TO *KILL* EACH OTHER.

KILL EACH OTHER ...AND I'LL BE *FREE*! RID OF THEM *BOTH*!

HAAA HA HA HA! *RID* OF THEM!

GONE. ALL, *ALL* GONE.

NO GREEN, NO GRAY, NO PINK WITH PURPLE POLKA DOTS.

US. US. JUST *US*.

HOW 'BOUT IF I LEAVE YOU GUYS *ALONE* FOR A WHILE.

HOW 'BOUT IF YOU *DO*.

A WHILE LATER...

OHHH, MAN. OH, IF ONLY I WERE *YOUNGER*...

OR IF *I* WERE ONLY *OLDER*...

MAKE MY *DAY*, STUD.

MAKE MY *LIFE*, SWEET CHILD.

SO, YOU GUYS LOOK... REFRESHED.

STOP *SMIRKING*, RICK.

THIS IS... INTERESTING.

IT'S KAL-KAN. *LOTS* CHEAPER, AND MEAT'S *MEAT*, RIGHT?

CRIPES! BETTY, STOP *CHOKING!* I WAS JUST *KIDDING*.

YOU PEOPLE ARE SO *SERIOUS* SOMETIMES.

MY NEW GIRLFRIEND'LL CHEER YOU RIGHT UP. SHE'S ON HER WAY OVER.

YOU'LL *LOVE* HER. I MET HER WHILE I WAS IN VEGAS.

VEGAS! HOW EXCITING! *ISN'T* IT, BRUCE?

OH... IMMENSELY.

I WAS TAKING ONE MORE SHOT AT A SINGING CAREER, AND OPENING FOR JOAN RIVERS AT THIS NEWLY REOPENED PLACE CALLED THE COLISEUM. THEY'D JUST RENOVATED AFTER SOME SORT OF TROUBLE *NO ONE* WOULD TALK ABOUT.

SO I MET THIS GIRL, AND WE HIT IT OFF *GREAT*.

BUT SHE HAD ALREADY MADE PLANS TO MOVE TO RENO. SHE'D BROKEN OFF WITH SOME GUY AND HAD SOURED ON VEGAS.

AND I FIGURED, HECK, I NEED A REGULAR PLACE *SOME*WHERE, RIGHT? SO I USED THE REST OF MY "SIDEKICKS" ADVANCE FOR THIS PLACE, AND...

HEY! I JUST HEARD A KNOCK. BET THAT'S *HER*.

VEGAS.

IT *COULDN'T* BE HER.

CHECK *THIS*, GUYS! I LANDED A *BIG* ONE THIS TIME.

OH, RICK, *STOP* IT.

GUYS, I WANT YOU TO MEET--

MARLO!

BRUCE!?

"BRUCE?!"

"MAR...LO?"

THIS IS *INSANITY!*

THIS IS THE KIND OF CRAZINESS THAT SEEMED TO FOLLOW JOE WHEREVER HE WENT! THAT'S WHY I BROKE UP WITH HIM!

AND RICK, YOU TOLD ME YOU *WEREN'T* INVOLVED WITH THEM ANYMORE! MASKED MYSTERY MEN AND SUPER-BEINGS AND PEOPLE LIKE THAT. YOU WERE GETTING *AWAY* FROM ALL THAT.

YEAH, WELL, NO MATTER WHERE I GO... THERE I AM.

RICK! HE'S DOWN *THERE!*

YOU'RE *REALLY* HIS WIFE? HOW LONG HAVE YOU TWO BEEN A COUPLE?

SINCE FOREVER.

HOW DO YOU *LIVE* WITH IT?

ONE DAY AT A TIME.

≷HUFF≷HUFF≷

YOU SHOULD *JOG* MORE.

SHUT UP!

HOLD IT, PEOPLE! KEEP *BACK!* THAT'S AN OR--

--DEERRRRRR...

I'M GONNA REGRET *THAT* MOVE BEFORE I GET MUCH OLDER.

KEEP GOING! *HURRY!*

BRUCE!

JOE!

ANY-BODY GOT A *THIRD* GUESS?

THEY'RE KILLING EACH OTHER, AND THEY'LL TAKE BRUCE *WITH* THEM! THEY DON'T CARE ABOUT *ANYTHING* EXCEPT THEIR *HATRED!*

BRUCE! PLEASE! *DO* SOMETHING!

BRUCE, *LISTEN* TO ME! YOU'RE *NOT* "PUNY BANNER"! YOU'RE *NOT* HELPLESS! YOU *CAN* BE *STRONG!*

PLEASE! HONEY! LOVER! FOR *ME!*

BE *STRONG!* PLEASE! BE *STRONG!*

WUUMF

Betty... did...

...it...

RICK... *YOU DON'T* TURN INTO SOME-ONE ELSE TOO, DO YOU?

SURE, ELVIS.

BRUCE... OH, DEAR LORD, WHAT DO WE DO *NOW?*

NOW? NOW WE GO TO WORK.

SORRY, WOULD'VE BEEN HERE SOONER, BUT I COULDN'T GET DECENT DIRECTIONS.

WHOA! *DOC SAMSON!*

NICE CAR.

THANKS, IT'S A RENTAL.

NEXT: WE'VE BEEN BUILDING TO IT FOR TWO YEARS, YOU MUST READ--

"Honey, I Shrunk the Hulk."

--CUT OUT FOR US.

BRUCE?

REALITY TO BRUCE... COME IN.

BRUCE, CAN YOU *HEAR* ME?

HE MAY HAVE TOTALLY WITH-DRAWN *INTO* HIMSELF. I'M TERRI-FIED WE MAY BE DOING MORE *HARM* THAN *GOOD*.

I UNDERSTAND YOUR CONCERNS, I'VE HYPNO-TIZED ENTIRE CROWDS WITH *NO* TROUBLE, BUT *THIS*...

THIS IS BEYOND *ANYTHING* I'VE EVER DEALT WITH. IT'S AMAZING.

WELL, AT LEAST YOU'RE LIVING UP TO YOUR REPUTATION FOR HYPNOTIC EXPERTISE, MAYNARD.

PLEASE, I PREFER "RING-MASTER." IF *YOUR* NAME WERE MAYNARD TIBOLDT, *YOU* WOULD, TOO.

IT WAS KIND OF THE WARDEN TO RELEASE ME INTO YOUR CUSTODY, ESPECIALLY SINCE I *SHOULDN'T* HAVE BEEN BEHIND BARS AT ALL.

THE MOST RECENT CRIMES MY CIRCUS COMMITTED WERE UTTERLY *WITHOUT* MY KNOWLEDGE.

I'M TRYING TO GIVE UP MY OLD LIFE. MAKE AMENDS. AND *THIS* IS A GOOD START. THE HULK AND I GO *WAY* BACK.

SUNGLASSES, DOCTOR? STILL WORRIED I'LL HYPNOTIZE YOU AND ESCAPE?

CALL IT CAUTION.

NOW BRING BRUCE UP TO A LEVEL I CAN *COMMUNICATE* WITH HIM AGAIN.

YOU'RE GOING *UNCONSCIONABLY* FAST, YOU KNOW. MOST MPD CASES TAKE MONTHS, EVEN *YEARS* OF THERAPY.

IN THE REAL WORLD...

THIS IS A NICE WAITING ROOM.

FOR A *HOSPITAL*, I MEAN. MY OLD ROOMMATE, SHE WORKED IN A HOSPITAL, AND IT WAS--

MISS CHANDLER...

CALL ME MARLO.

MISS CHANDLER, JUST WHAT WENT ON BETWEEN YOU AND BRUCE IN LAS VEGAS?

WE WERE JUST FRIENDS.

AND WHAT WENT ON BETWEEN YOU AND... WHAT WAS THE NAME... *JOE FIXIT?*

Oh.

LOOK, I CAN'T PRETEND I GET ALL THIS SCHIZO STUFF. I *BARELY* MADE IT THROUGH HIGH SCHOOL.

ALL I KNOW IS THAT JOE AND BRUCE ARE TWO DIFFERENT GUYS, AND *YOUR* GUY WAS LOYAL TO *YOU*, OKAY?

MRS. BANNER, YOU *GOTTA* TELL ME WHAT'S HAPPENING! WHAT DID YOU AND THE GREEN-HAIRED GUY *TALK* ABOUT?

BETTY, BRUCE IS WHAT WE REFER TO AS AN *MPD*-- MULTIPLE PERSONALITY DISORDER. THAT'S WHY THE VARIOUS CURES HAVEN'T TAKEN IN THE PAST. THEY AT-TACK THE *SYMPTOM*, BUT NOT THE *SOURCE*.

THE SOURCE IS WITHIN BRUCE'S *MIND*, AND WITH YOUR PERMISSION, WE'RE GOING TO *TREAT* IT.

AND WILL HE BE *NORMAL*?

HE CAN'T *EVER* BE "NORMAL", BETTY. HIS CELLS ARE GAMMA IRRADIATED. THAT WOULD *STILL* BE REFLECTED.

IF WE INTEGRATE THE PERSON-ALITIES, AS I *HOPE* TO, WHAT WE *WILL* GET IS A WHOLE BRUCE BANNER, FOR THE FIRST TIME IN *YEARS*.

ALL RIGHT, LEONARD. DO WHAT YOU THINK IS *BEST*.

LOOK, IF YOU DON'T WANT ME HERE FINE. I'LL--

OH, IT'S NOT *YOU*, IT'S ME. I'M BEING SUCH A *CREEP*, AND I--

ALL THESE YEARS, AND THEN HE'S *THIS* PERSON AND *THAT* PERSON AND I DON'T KNOW *WHO* I MARRIED AND--

SHH. LET IT OUT. IT'S OKAY.

OHHHH, MY LIFE IS SO... SO SCREWED ≥SOB≤ SCREWED UHHHHHHP.

HI. HOW YOU LADIES--?

RICK

HERE'S A TISSUE.

≥Sniff≤ Thangyu.

THE OL' RICK JONES TIMING STRIKES AGAIN. I'M OUTTA HERE.

"OKAY, SAMSON, I'VE GOT HIM UNDER AGAIN."

"BRUCE TELL ME WHAT YOU SEE."

mmmMMMMMmmm

mmm☀

LOOK, BRUCIE, ARE YOU INTERESTED IN DOING THIS OR *NOT?* YOU'RE A TWENTY YEAR OLD GUY AND YOU ACT LIKE YOUR HORMONES ARE STUCK IN *NEUTRAL.*

FRANKLY, SUSAN, I DON'T SEE THE *POINT* OF ALL THIS. THE GERMS ALONE ARE--

GERMS! THIS ISN'T ABOUT GERMS. WHAT'RE YOU, BRUCE, *AFRAID* OF ME?

I JUST HAVE *WORK* TO DO, THAT'S ALL. THIS IS COLLEGE, NOT A *PLAYPEN.*

YOU'D PROBABLY *PREFER* A PLAYPEN, WOULDN'T YOU? SO YOU COULD HAVE YOUR *THUMB* IN YOUR MOUTH INSTEAD OF *ME.*

THAT'S *UN-CALLED* FOR, SUSAN.

WHAT AM I, *UGLY?* YOU'RE AFRAID, THAT'S ALL. AFRAID TO GIVE A GIRL WHAT SHE *NEEDS* AND *WANTS* AND--

I GOT WHAT YOU WANT RIGHT *HERE,* BABE!

EEEEEPP!!

GET *AWAY!* GET *AWAY* FROM ME!

KEEP AWAY!

MONSTER!!

IT'S THE *CREATURE!* TAKE IT *AWAY!*

REBECCA BANNER

MAY SHE REST IN PEACE

BRUCE, DON'T YOU *UNDERSTAND?* WHAT *IS* IT? WHAT IS IT *REALLY?*

TAKE IT AWAY!

I *KNOW* YOU!!

YOU'RE MY HIDEOUS SON WHEN HE WAS A *BRAT!*

SINGLE-MINDED, *CHILDLIKE,* WANTING JUST TO BE LEFT ALONE!

AND YOU'RE HIM WHEN HE WAS IN *COLLEGE!* WANTING NOTHING BUT PLEASURE, A PERVERTED *MONSTER--!*

NO! IT *WASN'T* ME! IT WAS *YOU!*

YOU WERE THE MONSTER, FATHER!!

YOU WERE *INSANE.* SO CONVINCED THAT YOUR RADIATION WORK HAD GIVEN YOU A MUTANT MONSTER *SON.*

AND YOU *KILLED* MY MOTHER, AND I WAS SO *AFRAID...*

YOU GOT SO *MAD,* AND I SAW WHAT EMOTIONS *DID,* AND I... I WAS SO AF...*AFRAID...*

...OF BUH-BEING LIKE *YOU.*

SO...NO EMOTIONS, AND I...

≷CHOKE≷

I'D BE *SAFE.*

SAFE AND...

...AND CALM AND...AND...

...PUNY... I'M SO *PUNY*

...AND SO BAD... I'M...I'M SORRY, MA...

I'M SUH

I'M SUH

I'M SUHHHREEE

BACK TO REALITY...

AARRHHH

MOTHER!! WHAT'S HAPPENING!?

UH OH. HE'S TURNING INTO NORMAN BATES.

STOP MAKING JOKES AND BRING HIM OUT OF IT!

THIS IS BEYOND MY CONTROL TO BRING HIM OUT OF, SAMSON.

THIS IS BEYOND ANYTHING I'VE EVER SEEN.

THAT ANYONE'S EVER SEEN.

RICK, WHY ARE YOU LIMPING?

A KID *KICKED* ME IN THE SHIN. I'LL EXPLAIN LATER.

HOW LONG HAS IT *BEEN* ANYWAY?

TOO LONG. I'M *TIRED* OF WAITING.

I KNOW LEONARD SAID HE NEEDED PRIVACY, BUT ENOUGH'S *ENOUGH*.

I'M GOING *DOWN* THERE AND FINDING OUT WHAT'S GOING--

HONEY...

I'M HOME.

NEXT: OUR LITTLE CHRISTMAS TALE-- WILL BE A PRESENT FOR YOU-- IT FEATURES THE *GRAY HULK*-- AND THE *RHINO*, TOO!

ORIGINS...
Hulk

The Coming Of The Hulk

In 1962, just a few months after **Stan Lee** and **Jack Kirby** had seemingly struck comic book gold with the **Fantastic Four**, the powers that be at Marvel were demanding another new Super Hero title to add to their line-up. Choosing to go against any conceived Super Hero conventions, they created one of the most original characters to ever grace a comic book - the Incredible Hulk!

The initial inspiration for the Hulk came from Stan Lee's love of the classic horror movie **Frankenstein** and its misunderstood monster. He was intrigued by the idea of a hero who, like Frankenstein's monster, was essentially a good guy, but was hounded by the public due to his frightening appearance.

Another classic story influenced Lee as well - **Dr Jekyll and Mr Hyde**; the tale of a refined eighteenth century English gentleman who, after drinking a strange potion, was temporarily changed into an ugly, scheming and thoroughly evil-natured creature.

By combining elements of the two characters and adding a pinch of science fiction in the form of an experimental Gamma Bomb, Stan had got the character he wanted. He was good, but nobody knew it, and could also change suddenly from a man into a monster.

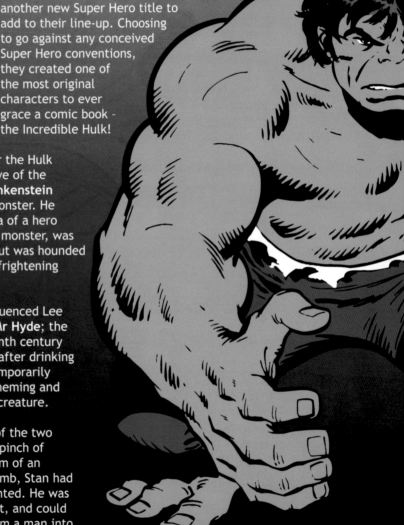

Though the Hulk seemed on the surface to be a simple brute, underneath there was so much more. In Lee's own words; "There's really so much more to it than just an angry monster, because he still has dim memories of his human self. In a way he hates Bruce Banner, because in a way Banner represents a weakling, where as the Hulk is all-powerful. So there's that dichotomy within him."

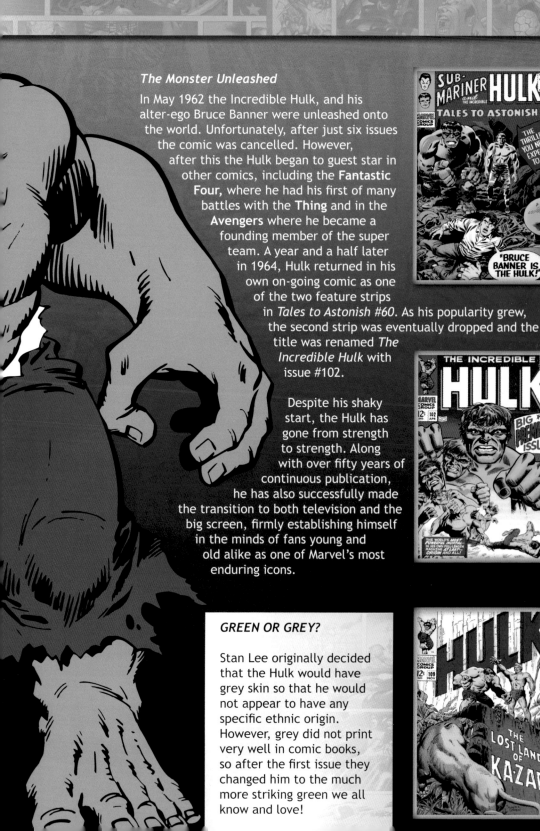

The Monster Unleashed

In May 1962 the Incredible Hulk, and his alter-ego Bruce Banner were unleashed onto the world. Unfortunately, after just six issues the comic was cancelled. However, after this the Hulk began to guest star in other comics, including the **Fantastic Four,** where he had his first of many battles with the **Thing** and in the **Avengers** where he became a founding member of the super team. A year and a half later in 1964, Hulk returned in his own on-going comic as one of the two feature strips in *Tales to Astonish #60.* As his popularity grew, the second strip was eventually dropped and the title was renamed *The Incredible Hulk* with issue #102.

Despite his shaky start, the Hulk has gone from strength to strength. Along with over fifty years of continuous publication, he has also successfully made the transition to both television and the big screen, firmly establishing himself in the minds of fans young and old alike as one of Marvel's most enduring icons.

GREEN OR GREY?

Stan Lee originally decided that the Hulk would have grey skin so that he would not appear to have any specific ethnic origin. However, grey did not print very well in comic books, so after the first issue they changed him to the much more striking green we all know and love!

THE WRITER

Peter David

Photo by
Luigi Novi

IF THERE is one name that is intimately linked with the story of the Incredible Hulk it is that of Peter David. Between 1987 and 1998, across an incredible 136 issues (not including spin-offs or annuals!), he truly made the Green Goliath his own.

But don't be misled; it isn't just David's longevity on the title that makes him so closely associated with the Hulk. In fact, that's the lesser of his achievements. What makes his involvement so integral to Ol' Greenskin's current high standing is the wealth of nuances and innovations he brought to the character. When he took over Incredible Hulk in 1987 he chose to embrace over a quarter of a century's history. But unlike many writers who have found themselves weighed down by the vast amount baggage that lengthy continuity brings with it, he nimbly managed to avoid all the usual clichés.

The biggest challenge he set himself was how to handle the Hulk/Bruce Banner metamorphosis and to explain why the gamma-irradiated scientist's transformations weren't stable – why they could result in radically different versions of the jade behemoth. He brought subtlety and depth to a misunderstood creature that was mainly envisaged as a monosyllabic raging monster whose most famous utterances are "Hulk smash!", "Hulk the strongest one there is!" and "The madder Hulk gets, the stronger Hulk gets!"

Looking back on his highly regarded run, Peter David has commented, "I didn't think it was that big a deal. I figured I would be on the series for six months, maybe a year. I had no idea I'd be on it for 12 years."

The storyline dubbed Silent Screams ran through Incredible Hulk #370-377, beginning 40 issues into David's reign on the title. Along the way David had already worked wonders with the Grey Hulk (last seen in 1963's historic Incredible Hulk #1). This tricky, manipulative and ego-centric incarnation of the Hulk had been restored to the Marvel Universe by Al Milgrom in #324 [1986], he had since relocated to Las Vegas, adopted the name Joe Fixit, became a morally ambiguous enforcer and tough guy and gained a new girlfriend in Marlo Chandler.

It was all part of the writer's grand plan, which reached its climax in #377. However, David says

HMMM, LITTLE JACK REMINDS ME OF ME AT THAT AGE.

AND NOT JUST IN LOOKS, HE'S SO QUIET AND WITHDRAWN,

he was building off the idea put forward by another writer, Bill Mantlo, although Barry Windsor-Smith claims he initially brought Marvel the concept of Banner's tortured and abusive infancy being at the root of his monstrous rages. "My tweak on it was I believed that – as a result of this childhood abuse – Bruce Banner was a perfect candidate for Multiple Personality Disorder; the notion being that even if he hadn't been hit by gamma rays, sooner or later he still would have suffered from MPD, and that the Hulk was simply a gamma-irradiated manifestation of a condition that actually exists.

"It also," he continued, "explained, to my mind, why the Hulk had undergone a variety of changes throughout the years in terms of his personality and attitudes: we were seeing other personalities, just like your standard issue MPD. To me this was a concept rife with possibilities, and it was never

really pursued after Bill introduced the concept in Hulk #314. Mantlo established in #314 – possibly via Windsor-Smith – that Bruce Banner was abused as a child. I'm the one who took it to the next step and said that childhood abuse resulted in him developing Multiple Personality Disorder. That subsequently led to the storyline in which the Hulk was merged, because that is, theoretically, how they deal with MPD."

Silent Screams was the result of almost four years' groundwork but David was not content to coast from there. Rightly regarded as the Green Goliath's foremost scribe, he continued to work his creative magic on the Hulk until he left the title in 1998. However, he returned for a brief eleven issue run on Hulk in 2004, but had to reluctantly leave the title once again due to other work commitments. He also made another foray into the world of green-skinned, gamma-powered heroes in 2008, this time writing 17 issues of the Hulk's sister title She-Hulk.

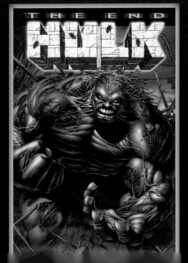

Of the many Hulk one-shots Peter David has written, his most famous is probably *Hulk: The End*, a post-apocalyptic tale designed to be the final Hulk story. Reunited with artist Dale Keown once again, the story has become a modern classic and is considered a fitting end to the Hulk saga.

THE ARTIST
Dale Keown

THE STORY you hold in your hands propelled Canadian rock 'n' roller Dale Keown out of obscurity and transformed him into a comicbook superstar.

Born in Grand Prairie, Alberta on July 23, 1962, the bass-playing artist taught himself to draw between gigs while touring with his band. His first professional assignment came in 1986 for **Aircel Publishing.**

He followed up on *Dragonring #9* with a handful more issues of that series, as well as working on the Ottawa-based outfit's titles

Elford, Samurai, Dragon Force (which he also wrote) and *Warlock 5*. When Aircel was absorbed into **Malibu Graphics' Eternity Comics** imprint in 1988, he continued with *Dragon Force*. He also contributed covers to such titles as *Dinosaurs for Hire, The New Humans, Beach Party* and *The Walking Dead*, a 1989 four-parter, not to be confused with Robert Kirkman's far more high profile title from Image Comics and its hugely popular TV spin-off. His big break came in late 1989, when he was commissioned to draw *Nth Man, the Ultimate Ninja #8*. Though it was just a fill-in issue for a relatively obscure Marvel title, it opened the door to bigger and better assignments from the House of Ideas. Not only did he gain a regular gig as *Savage She-Hulk* cover artist but also another fill in... on *Incredible Hulk #367*.

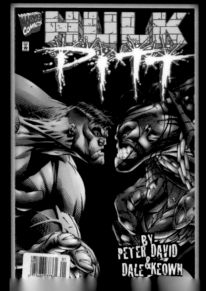

With #369 he became the regular penciller on the Green Goliath's title, joining series writer **Peter David** for 26 issues. It was that collaboration across almost two-and-a-half years that took Keown from the sidelines of the black and white indie press to comicdom's centre stage.

In less than four years he had gone from the sidelines to top of the bill. Now much in demand, he was lured from Marvel to **Image Comics,** a publishing co-operative set up in 1990 by other big name artists. There he was offered the chance to produce a creator-owned title. The result was **Pitt,** a Hulk-like extraterrestrial warrior pursued to Earth by other super powered aliens.

Launched to great success at the very end of 1992, Keown released 9 issues of Pitt with Image, then decided to publish under his own **Full Bleed Studios** banner. Also at this time he

got back together with Peter David for a Marvel 52-pager, 1997's *Hulk/Pitt*. Full Bleed released 11 issues of Pitt – as well as five of *Pitt Crew*, a spin-off title to which he contributed covers –but by the end of 1999 Keown was out of the publishing game.

The Canadian artist didn't resurface until mid-2001, when he began producing covers, initially for **DC** but also subsequently for Marvel, where he reunited again with David for *Incredible Hulk: The End*, an out of continuity 2002 one-shot for which the duo provided a coda in 2006's Giant-Size *Incredible Hulk #1*.

As 2002 closed, Keown began to draw The Darkness for Image's **Top Cow** imprint. He pencilled just the first six issues of the 2002 series but followed it up in 2004 with *The Darkness/Incredible Hulk* one-shot and then five years later with the three-issue *Darkness/Pitt*. Both were published by Image/Top Cow for which he also now draws covers.

These days Keown lives in Toronto where he concentrates almost entirely on covers and pinups, making only the occasional foray into storytelling. With over 20 years of highly-regarded artwork under his belt, the Canadian artist remains one of the major comicbook talents to emerge in the last decade of the 20th century.

MOVIE MASTERPIECE

Dale Keown's rendition of the Hulk is so iconic that in 2003 he was asked to create a large portion of the artwork used on collectable memorabilia for Ang Lee's HULK movie.

ARTIST'S GALLERY

Hulk

Throughout his lifetime, various accidents and strange occurrences have caused Bruce Banner's muscular, gamma-enhanced alter-ego to appear in different forms. Below are just a few of the Hulk's most famous manifestations.

Original Grey Hulk
Art By Jack Kirby

Grey "Mr Fixit" Hulk
Art By Dale Keown

Banner-less Hulk
Art By Mike Deodato Jr

Intelligent Hulk
Art by Dale Keown

House of M Incarnation
(Alternative Universe Hulk)
Art By Jorge Lucas

Maestro
*(A possible
evil future
incarnation
of the Hulk)*
Art By George
Perez

Gladiator Hulk
(from Planet Hulk)
Art by Ladronn

FURTHER READING

If you've enjoyed the style and art in this graphic novel, you may be interested in exploring some of these books too.

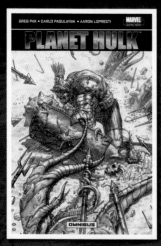

The Incredible Hulk: Planet Hulk

Volumes 45 & 46 of the Ultimate Marvel Graphic Novels Collection

At the book shop:
ISBN: 9781905239665

Fall Of The Hulks

At the book shop:
ISBN: 9781846534621

World War Hulk

Volume 55 of the Ultimate Marvel Graphic Novels Collection

At the book shop:
ISBN: 9781905239771

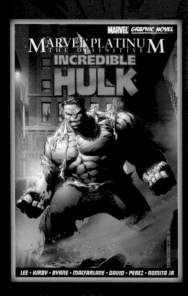

Marvel Platinum: The Definitive Hulk

At the book shop:
ISBN: 9781905239887

The Incredible Hulk: Banner and The End

At the book shop:
ISBN: 9781904159254

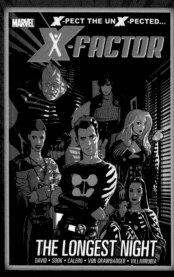

X-Factor: The Longest Night

At the book shop:
ISBN: 0785118179